The Disappearing Spoon
Study Guide

Pembroke Notes

First published by Dog Ear Publishing
4010 W. 86th Street, Ste H
Indianapolis, IN 46268
www.dogearpublishing.net

ISBN: 978-1-4575-2325-0

This book is printed on acid-free paper.

Printed in the United States of America

INTRODUCTION

I have been teaching since 1994 with a background in elementary, special education, and secondary English. I have always been passionate about the role reading has in the learning process. In the perfect world all students would be avid readers and life-long learners. They would all blossom as individuals, cultivate knowledge, thinking and communication skills, and integrate into the real world with active voices.

I believe the English class is each student's gateway for discovering how he/she relates to language, literature, ideas, and the world. They need to read proficiently, write effectively, and critique the media that surrounds them. All materials used to master these skills should be effective and engaging while promoting critical thinking skills.

At a recent visit to the local teacher store in my hometown, I realized that 99% of the support materials supplied for the professional focused on the PreK-6 grade students. Little was available for the high school English teacher. This was when I decided to help the high school student as well as the high school teacher by sharing my study guides and notes on informational texts. This seems especially timely when states, school districts, and schools are faced with new standards that emphasize a focus on nonfiction. You will find all my materials meet the Common Core and Alaska standards.

CHAPTER 1

Pgs. 23-31

1. Why was antimony great for building custom acids?

2. Why couldn't you pick up a substance with a pH of -31?

3. What is carborane good for?

4. Lewis's work was passed over for _____?

5. What possibilities could have contributed to Lewis's death?

6. What elements lie in the "great plains" of the periodic table?

7. Sodium has _____ electrons; magnesium has _____ electrons.

8. Transition metals appear in columns _____ through _____ of the periodic table and rows _____ through _____.

9. Lanthanides are also called the _____ _____.

10. Why isn't it possible to find a pure sample of a lanthanide in nature?

11. What makes up 99% of an atom's mass?

12. Write a paragraph about the difficulties Maria Goeppert had to overcome to become a recognized as a scientist.

13. She began work in 1948 on the _____, the core and essence of an atom. The _____ _____ determines the atom's identity.

14. The atomic number plus the number of _____ is called the _____ _____.

15. Explain the mystery that Goeppert-Mayer discovered.

16. Filling   nuclear   shells   leads   to _____.

17. She proved that nuclei do have shells and do form what she called _____ nuclei. The magic happens at atomic numbers _____, _____, _____, _____, _____, _____, and so on.

18. Why is oxygen in seemingly overabundance?

19. Beautiful shapes are _____ _____.

20. What happened in 1963?

21. Why is reading the periodic table up and down or longitudinal more significant than reading from left to right?

CHAPTER 2

1. What does the longest word mean, discovered in what year, and how many letters?

2. Describe the most versatile element on the periodic table.

3. Each amino acid contains _____ atoms on one end, a _____ on the other, and a trunk of _____ atoms in the middle.

4. What allows carbon to build complex chains and why are the bonds steady and stable?

5. What was the 189,819 –letter- protein shortened to?

6. What element has been cited as a carbon-based life in other galaxies?

7. What is the relationship between silicon and an alien?

8. What is P16 and how does it develop?

9. What is the most common mineral on earth?

10. What is the relationship between volcanoes and dinosaurs?

11. What is a "fractious word"?

12. What do advances in artificial intelligence tell us about the brain?

13. Why wouldn't silicon work as a substitute for carbon in forms of life?

14. What would the environment look like if it were silicon based instead of carbon?

15. While an element may resemble the one below it, _____ _____ accumulate.

16. What element is like the "black sheep of the family?"

17. In a short paragraph describe how the semiconductor industry came to be. Include William Shockley.

18. Who are Bardeen and Brattain and how did they have a symbiotic relationship?

19. Why did B & B use germanium?

20. Explain Shockley's belief in eugenics.

21. Shockley was ruthless. How did he break up the B & B team?

22. Why did things turn sour for germanium?

23. P.T. Barnum is a metaphor for whom? What did he do?

23. What is a gaffe?

25. What was the job of low-paid women at TI?

26. What did Jack Kilby change? When did he finally get recognition?

27. What did Sir Isaac Newton say?

28. Who became the father of the periodic table?

CHAPTER 3

1. Bunsen's first love was _____.

2. Roman assassins used it to _____.

3. What is a cacodyl?

4. What is the best antidote to arsenic and how does it work?

5. After Bunsen became blind he transferred his interest to _____ . What did he construct in his lab?

6. What ensured Bunsen scientific immortality?

7. If a mysterious substance emits red, yellowish green, baby blue, and indigo blue bands what does it contain?

8. What is Bunsen's second great contribution to the periodic table?

9. How does the periodic table and "The Odyssey" compare?

10. How did Mendeleev's mother help with her son's career?

11. Mendeleev and Meyer split what medal?

12. What 3 things did Mendeleev have a hard time believing in?

13. _____ are the most ambiguous and knotty elements to place on the table?

14. Why did Mendeleev mesmerize people?

15. Explain why Dostoevsky and Mendeleev were considered outsized characters.

16. What did the tsar say about a double standard for Mendeleev?

17. How does Mendeleev's work compare to Darwin and Einstein's work?

18. Who discovered gallium?

19. What characteristics of gallium make it a good practical joke?

20. Using context clues define acrimonious.

21. What makes a great story?

22. What does Einstein say about discovery?

23. What were a couple of mistakes Mendeleev made?

24. How could Mendeleev have solved his frustration about cerium?

25. Why was Johann Friedrich Botteger treated like Rumplestiltskin?

26. Describe the power of porcelain.

27. What were the secret ingredients of Chinese porcelain?

28. What is Ytterby?

29. Bright colors are dead giveaways of _____.

30. Scandinavians embraced rationalism en masse. What does this mean?

31. What elements did Gandolin discover?

CHAPTER 4
Pgs. 65-71

1. Prior to 1939 what was the common view of the origin of elements?

2. What discovery in 1939 began to dissolve the above theory?

3. What is technetium and where does it exit?

4. What is B2FH?

5. When do things really start shaking?

6. There is an interesting metaphor at the bottom of page 66 that explain the change in star matter. What is the metaphor?

7. When stars die what do they create?

8. B2FH traces various fusion reactions and explains the recipe for producing everything up to iron; it's nothing less than _____.

9. Once iron is spotted in a star, it's safe to assume

10. Iron is the final _____

11. According to B2FH where do the heaviest elements, twenty-seven through ninety-two, _____through_____ come from?

12. Explain in a short paragraph how elements develop in a super-nova.

13. What happened 4.6 billion years ago?

14. How were the giant planets like Jupiter formed?

15. Why is Uranus misnamed?

16. What is the Shoemaker-Levy 9 comet?

17. What effect did the Hale-Bopp comet have on Earth?

18. What did scientists hope was at the center of Jupiter's core?

19. What are contained in the black oceans of Jupiter?

20. Why do elements have strange lives on Jupiter?

21. What is the giant red eye?

22. What is the basic elemental composition of real stars?

23. Why is there an abundance of helium and neon toward the center of Jupiter?

CHAPTER 4

Pgs. 72-80

1. What are the solar system's rocky planets?

2. Define <u>coalesce.</u>

3. How did healthy deposits of all elements form on the planets?

4. What is at the core of each planet?

5. How do the planets in our solar system differ from the planets around other stars?

6. Each solar system has a unique _____ _____.

7. The number below each element on the periodic table indicates its _____ _____, the number of _____ plus the number of _____.

8. How have scientists deduced the earth was formed?

9. Who help fix the date of the planet through experiments on lead and uranium?

10. What two isotopes does uranium break down?

11. What would Patterson have to do to go back to the year zero?

12. What are preserved hunks of primordial earth?

13. Meteors are solid _____.

14. Where did Patterson get meteor bits to conduct his experiments?

15. Why did Pb, lead ruin Patterson's early attempts to analyze meteors?

16. How did he treat lead to keep out of his space rocks?

17. What about the lead from your hair?

18. What was the metaphor Patterson used for humanity?

19. What is the result of Patterson becoming an activist?

20. Venus, Mercury, and Mars were formed simultaneously. What does that mean?

21. What were Luis and Walter Alvarez's discovery?

22. Iridium is a siderophile. What is that and where is it found?

23. Besides dinosaurs what else was destroyed 65 million years ago?

24. When was the asteroid-iridium extinction theory seemingly proved?

25. Did all dinosaurs die out at the same time? Explain.

26. What is the chance of an asteroid passing close to the sun hitting our planet?

27. What is the theory about the sun and a companion star?

28. What is the relationship between Nemesis and rhenium?

29. What simile was used to describe critics on the Nemisis theory? (bottom of pg. 78)

30. What is the nearest star and how far is it from earth?

31. What is the counter argument against Copernican revolution?

32. What is an Oort cloud?

33. What does Eric Scerri write?

34. What does Carl Sagan say about life?

35. Besides genius what does higher concentrations of rare elements inspire?

CHAPTER 5

1. We can trace chemical warfare back to _____,
    which used _____.

2. Define harbinger

3. The _____ of 1899 banned
    chemical weapons in war.

4. Why did the United States refuse to sign this pact?

5. _____ was secretly chosen as a chemical weapon
    because it irritates the eyes and nose. This agent was a
    _____ so potent it could incapacitate a
    grown man with hot searing tears.

6. _____ _____ was one of the great minds in
    the history of chemistry when he figured out how to convert
    _____ in air – into an industrial product.

7. The one important thing nitrogen does is
    _____.

8. What are the steps Haber used to capture nitrogen?

9. We can thank him for feeding most of the world's _____ bil-
    lion people today.

10. What was the real reason Haber pursued this line of experimentation?

11. These were the types of explosives _____ used to blow a hole in a _____ in _____.

12. Like petty _____ who twist scientific innovations into efficient killing devices, Haber's story is darker because he was _____.

13. How did Germany deal with Haber's Jewish heritage?

14. How did Germany get by the Hague pact?

15. Why did Haber change from the use of bromine to chlorine?

16. How does chlorine gas affect the human body?

17. What is Haber's Rule?

18. How did Haber's wife react to Fritz's scientific work?

19. What was the irony of Huber's Nobel Prize of 1919?

20. What happened to Haber when Germany lost the war?

21. How did the Nazis treat Haber?

22. _____ would go on to become the "it" metal of the Second World War.

23. What are Big Berthas?

24. Why was molybdenum a good addition to steel in weaponry?

25. How and why did the Japanese learn about this metal recipe?

26. How did a Germany mining company come to own a molybdenum mine in Colorado and why?

27. What is the relationship between Otis King and Two-Gun Adams?

28. What was the relationship between Metallgesellschaft and American Metal?

29. W or wolfram stands for _____.

30. Who supplied the Axis powers with tungsten during the war?

31. What was the theory behind Antonio Salazar supplying tungsten to both sides?

32. Once added to steel it made excellent _____, _____, and _____ that could take down tanks.

33. How did the Nazis pay for the tungsten?

34. Explain why the US disagreed with Winston Churchill.

35. When did Salazar issue a full tungsten embargo on Germany?

36. What did Rhett Butler say about the making of fortunes?

37. Every metal has a niche:
Gadolinium

Neodymium

Scandium

38. Describe the 2 myths that tantalum and niobium were named after.

39. Tantalum and niobium are vital for making _____.

40. Why did supplying coltan cause more problems in the Congo?

41. What is one reason the killing of gorillas came about?

43. Why is tin now a major problem for the Congo?

44. What did Joseph Conrad say about the Congo?

45. More than _____ people have died in the Congo since the mid 1990s.

CHAPTER 6

1. Why have some species of elements gone extinct?

2. What simile describes Henry Mosley's dedication to his work?

3. How did Mosley feel about foreigners at Manchester?

4. Describe in a sentence or two how X-rays are formed?

5. What are the seven holes in the table?

6. Explain the meeting between Georges Urbain and Moseley.

7. What was the "one of the most hideous and most irreparable crimes in history"?

8. Explain what, where, and when element sixty-one was discovered.

9. Who was it named after?

10. What was the famous offspring of plutonium and uranium?

11. How did Luis Alvarez react to Otto Hahn's experiments on _____?

12. What was the tool devised to understand how subatomic particles behaved?

13. What is the field of radioactivity?

14. What is the most powerful atomic "shrapnel"?

15. Explain Alpha decay and Beta decay.

16. What did Leo Szilard patent?

17. Why did a few undiscovered elements remain undiscovered?

18. What strategy did the Manhattan Project adopt?

19. Why was it important to know how much plutonium and uranium was needed to make a bomb?

20. What was meant by "building bombs numerically"? What were the "computers"?

21. The Ulam –and- von -Neumann form of probability of numbers was eventually called the _____.

22. What are "supers"?

23. Why is a cobalt-60 dirty bomb and what kinds of damage can it do?

24. Explain the difference in radiation in the nuclear bomb and the dirty bomb.

25. What are the long- term effects of Cobalt 60 in the earth?

26. How long would it take for the land to recover?

27. What was the theme of the movie, "Dr. Strangelove"?

28. What is MAD?

29. What happened between the Soviet Union and the United States at the end of this chapter?

CHAPTER 7

1. What were scientists doing in the laboratories that ended in being a "bitter creation?"

2. What was the element created by Edwin McMillan?

3. How were scientists used during WWII?

4. What circumstances led Seaborg to conduct science that discovered the element with a +7 charge named _____?

5. What was the relationship between Glenn Seaborg and Al Ghiorso?

6. What job did Seaborg give Ghiorso?

7. What metaphor does the author use to describe the success of discovering elements by Ghiorso and Seaborg?

8. What are alpha particles? What are their advantages over neutrons?

9. What happened when alphas struck plutonium?

10. The 2 new elements were named _____ and _____.

11. Why did Ghiorso want to give chemical symbol Bm to berkelium?

12. What was element 99 and 100 and where were they discovered?

13. Why was there disagreement in naming element 101 mendelevium?

14. What were elements 102 and 103, their names, and who they were named after?

15. What two elements were discovered in Russia?

16. What were the reasons that Russia never had the scientific genius as others had?

17. Explain the October Revolution that occurred in November.

18. How was fluorine a benefit to public health? What did the John Birch Society think about this?

19. What did Lysenko falsely claim under Russia's Stalin?

20. How did Stalin treat scientists?

21. What is black snow?

22. Why were physicists left in peace under Stalin?

23. What happened to the 650 scientists of the elite Academy of Sciences?

24. How was Flyorov able to gain his own lab under Stalin?

25. What is "blackboard science"?

26. What is IUPAC and what did it arbitrate?

27. What are elements 104 to 109?

28. Victor Ninov caused controversy. Why?

CHAPTER 8

1. Who was the greatest element craftsman of an earlier era who nabbed the most slippery and elusive element on the entire table?

2. What was Segre's nationality?

3. Segre wrote Pauling for advice on experiments with _____.

4. _____, _____, and _____ were all mistakes.

5. Serendipitous, clumsiness, and outright blunders have pushed science ahead all through history. What does serendipitous mean?

6. No element has been discovered for the "first time" more times than _____ _____.

7. What element did Masataka Ogawa nam that was reexamined in 2004?

8. Why had a continent-wide plot risen to discredit the Germans?

9. Why had element 43 proved so elusive?

10. Ernest Lawrence invented an atom smasher called a _____.

11. Segre heard that the cyclotron used replaceable _____ parts.

12. Describe Walter Noddack's visit with Segre.

13. Lawrence was obtuse with people. What does obtuse mean?

14. What consequential discovery did Enrico Fermi miss?

15. Segre later became a _____ as well as a hunter of
_____.

16. Who were the women who clearly discovered fission?

17. What is nature's first forbidden element?

18. During 1925 _____ was the center of the scientific universe.

19. Pauling proved to be the _____ of chemistry. Whom is this referring?

20. Pauling   proved   "that   chemistry   could   be
_____   rather   than   being
_____,"

21. Why are snowflakes six sided?

22. Why does sickle-cell anemia kill people?

23. Pauling also showed how proteins could form long cylinders called _____.

24. The study of _____ was a step up in sophistication from creating new elements.

25. Explain the discovery of DNA in 1869.

26. Linus Pauling's son, Peter, worked in the same lab as
    _____ and _____.

27. _____ shows the shapes of mole-
    cules.

28. _____ are the mirror image of reg-
    ular protons: have a negative charge, may travel backward in time,
    and scarily, will annihilate any "real" matter such as you and me,
    on contact.

CHAPTER 9

After reading chapter 9 add details to each topic.

Kamioka mines

Itai-itai

Norboru Hagino

Godzilla

Big Four Pollution Diseases

Mimic

Graham Frederick Young

Fidel Castro

Knick-knack

Half- life

Medicinal

Noble metal

David Hahn

Breeder reaction

CHAPTER 10

After reading chapter 10 add details to each topic.

Obscure (not well known) elements

Antiseptic powers

Copper

Oligodynamic

Vanadium

Mt. Fuji

Gadolinium

MRI—Tumors

Side effects

Silver

The Blue Man

Stan Jones—Y2K

Handedness

Tartaric acid—Louis Pasteur

Gerhard Domagk—prontosil

IGF—FDR—Sulfonamide

Hitler

Chiral chemicals

Thalidomide

William Knowles

Catalysts

Oliver Sacks—L-dopa—Awakenings—Volcano metaphor

CHAPTER 11

After reading chapter 11 add details to each topic.

Handbook of Chemistry and Physics

Space shuttle Columbia

Apollo 1

Pure oxygen

Inert nitrogen

John Bjornstad, Forest Cole

Kills with kindness

Per-Ingvar Branemark, femurs of rabbits, titanium, prosthetics

Osteoblasts

Collagen

Touch, taste, smell

Tellurium

Beryllium

Miraculin

Sour

Gymnema sylvestre

Gandhi, iodine, Salt March to Dandi

Hypochondriacs, iodized salt, government

Goiter, thyroid, hormones

Bertrand Russell, chemistry through and through

CHAPTER 12

1. No less than a scientific (history), there's a _____ of the elements.

2. Why is Poland compared to a cheap theater set?

3. What were some obstacles standing in the way of Marie Sklodowska's scientific education?

4. Marie's work on _____, the heaviest natural metal provided a crucial insight: _____.

5. What was the species whose population exploded during the twentieth century?

6. Why was Curie studying pitchblende?

7. What was the element named that Marie Curie discovered? Why was it named this?

8. What was the scandal caused by Curie and Paul Langevin? How did it end?

9. Curie had a _____ reputation. What is this?

10. Why could polonium be a mocking metaphor for Poland?

11. Describe a Radithor?

12. What happened to Alexander Litvinenko?

13. What was considered Irene Joliot-Curie and Frederic Joliot-Curie work?

14. Why was the death of Irene Curie ironic?

15. How did Hevesy waste 2 years of time?

16. How does the Geiger counter and Hevesy's dinner relate?

17. Who was Niels Bohr?

18. What started as a scientific argument and became a political dispute about territory and boundaries? To what is this referring?

19. What does "stinks of Huns" have to do with a Nobel Prize?

20. Describe the dire problems Hevesy faced besides his Nobel Prize?

21. How did Hitler overlook the gold medals?

22. Why was "brevium" changed to "protactinium?"

23. Who discovered element 91?

24. Why was Meitner smitten with Hahn?

25. What did Hitler do in 1933?

26. Why did Meitner's world collapse?

27. Why didn't Hahn receive the Nobel Prize in 1943?

28. Should Hahn have received the Nobel Prize in 1944 alone? Explain your answer.

29. Element _____ now and forever will be known as _____.

30. Who was this named after?

C-13

Pgs. 223-228

1. The history of money is tangled with the history of _____.

2. Throughout history what have passed for currency?

3. Describe the myth called Midas.

4. Describe the kingdom of the real Midas.

5. Bronze metals differ depending on the percentages of _____, _____, and other elements where the metals were mined.

6. Zinc mixed with copper forms _____.

7. Describe the difference in look of brass and bronze.

8. Brass was passed as _____ in Midas's kingdom.

9. What is the difference between the dream of finding gold and a real gold rush?

10. What is fool's gold?

11. Discribe the gold rush of the Outback.

12. Describe tellurides.

13. Some tellurium compounds smell pungent, _____.

14. Why did "hell finally break loose"?

15. Relate Kalgoorlie and the Golden Mile.

16. The first real money, coins made of _____ in _____. King _____ figured out how to separate _____ into silver and gold coins, establishing a _____system.

17. Describe the counterfeiting of King Polycrates.

18. Today, counterfeiting is considered _____, but for most of history it was considered _____. Convicted could receive _____.

CHAPTER 13

229-237

1. What was Newton employment at the end of the 1600s?

2. Endemic means common in a particular place. What form of counterfeiting was endemic in seedier parts of London?

3. How did William Chaloner pay for his crime of counterfeiting?

4. What were the advantages of paper money over coins?

5. Why is the situation vice versa these days?

6. Metals like _____ helps governments combat swindling.

7. What determines the colors of light?

8. What is the difference between normal emissions of light and florescence?

9. How does the EU help prevent counterfeiting?

10. Why is that (color) shift useful?

11. Explain why there are two euros in each banknote.

12. Describe Primo Levi's currency and how it was used?

13. How was The Wonderful Wizard of Oz an allegory?

14. Ounce-by-ounce, the most valuable element, among elements you can actually buy is _____.

15. How did Paul McCartney celebrate becoming the bestselling musician of all time?

16. Why did aluminum cap the Washington Monument?

17. Who was the "aluminum boy wonder"?

18. What was one of the most successful business ventures in history?

19. How rich was Hall when he died in 1914?

20. Money _____.

CHAPTER 14

1. As science became more sophisticated what dictated when, if, and how science got done?

2. Why were the rich exploring sciences?

3. Why based on the above answer were the elements named as they were?

4. Who was considered by many to be the most accomplished German ever to live?

5. Explain the imagery of a Quasimodo-like job.

6. Using context clues what does epochal mean?

7. Define <u>dilettante.</u>

8. Goethe's novel <u>Elective Affinities </u>was written as a metaphor for_____.

9. What is the difference between Neptunists and Plutonists?

10. Why would Goethe be crushed today?

11. What were some differences between Goethe and J. W. Dobereiner?

12. What element is Dobereiner associated with?

13. What are triads? Give 2 examples.

14. What are the Dobereiner's pillars?

15. What made Dobereiner famous?

16. "The history of science is_____."

17. How does the periodic table according to Goethe resemble art?

18. According to the text what is the difference between forced obsolescence and artificial obsolescence?

19. What was Kenneth Parker famous for?

20. What was used for the tips of his new pens?

21. As design prophet Moholy-Nagy could have predicted, _____ trumped _____.

22. What was an amazing feat in 1947?

23. Why did the high-end market for Parker 51 begin to shrivel?

24. What was the irony about Mark Twain, the pen, and the typewriter?

25. How did Mark Twain and Goethe feel about humans and their use of technology?

26. According to this author how would Mark Twain feel about technology had he lived another 40 years?

27. Describe Robert Lowell's personality.

28. What did pharmaceutical psychology say about Lowell?

29. How does lithium help someone with depression?

30. What is the difference between so called "normal" people and those with bipolar disorders?

31. How do people with "pathological enthusiasm" act?

31. What are the "black dogs"?

32. _____ resets the proteins over and over.

33. What is the down side of artists taking lithium?

34. Lowell's lithium may be a case where it provided _____ but subdued _____, and made a mad _____ merely _____.

CHAPTER 15

1. According to this author what are the differences between mad artists and mad scientists?

2. What spurred Crookes to take up the new movement of spiritualism?

3. Crookes compared himself to a traveler in exotic lands, a _____ of the paranormal.

4. Explain the relationship between selenium and 1) AIDS, 2) cattle

5. Crookes was the first to suggest the existence of _____.

6. How do pathological scientists work?

7. Why does our author call paleontology pathological science?

8. What did the HMS Challenger dredge up from the ocean floor?

9. What did paleontologists determine just from the teeth?

10. Why could some call this faulty science?

11. Sailors' eyewitness accounts of megalodons are unreliable. Why?

12. What argument does people make about the possible existence of megalodons?

13. What did Pons and Fleischmann think they had discovered when they used a palladium electrode in a current of water?

14. This discovery basically implied that the world's energy problems were _____.

15. The two scientists appealed directly to President George H. W. Bush for _____ in immediate research funds.

16. In reality the duo had overlooked _____ _____ and used faulty _____ _____.

17. Why did their work turn into pathological science?

18. Why did Rontgen think he had gone stark mad?

19. How did he skirt pathological science?

20. What had he discovered?

21. Why was Rontgen every scientist's hero?

22. Element #111 became _____.

CHAPTER 16

1. What does extreme cold do to the elements?

2. What was the disappointment to Robert Scott when he reached the South Pole?

3. What conditions did Scott face on this journey?

4. What did he notice about his fuel containers?

5. What happened to his team?

6. What happens to pure tin chemically when it is faced with extreme cold?

7. At what cold temperature does tin start reacting?

8. Why is this condition sometimes called "tin leprosy"?

9. What are 2 examples of the above condition happening?

10. Why is Jell-O called a hybrid state of matter?

11. Describe how ice has several states of matter.

12. What was the first noble gas compound created by Neil Bartlett?

13. When was the first krypton solid created?

14. _____ wears the title belt for the single hardest element humans have forced into a compound.

15. How are atoms arranged differently in solids, liquids, and gases?

16. Explain simply the law of electricity.

17. What happens to the electrical current at -450 degrees in a super-conductor?

18. Who was the BCS theory of superconductivity named after?

19. What is wave-particle duality?

20. Lasers use crystals of _____ spiked with _____.

21. What metaphor is used to describe the action of a laser?

22. Laser beams are so powerful they can induce _____, yet so focused they can _____.

23. What 2 big names called Charles Townes discovery of masers and then laser impossible?

24. So as physicists have done throughout history, Bose decided to pretend _____, admit that _____, and _____.

25. Temperature just measures _____. Hot molecules are _____, and cold molecules_____.

26. Scientists might soon be able to build _____ that shoot out ultra-focused beams of atoms thousands of times more powerful than light laser.

CHAPTER 17

1. One of the most important pieces of scientific equipment in history was invented by a _____.

2. Bubbles in liquids form around _____ or _____.

3. Bubbles in beer are dissolved pockets of _____.

4. When do kaons, muons, and pions appear?

5. Liquids are thousands of time denser than _____.

6. Glaser invented the _____.

7. Liquid hydrogen boils at _____, so even minute amounts of heat with make a _____.

8. What do biologists use bubbles to study?

9. What is foam?

10. Calcium-enriched bone are both _____ yet _____.

11. Rainwater and calcium form _____.

12. English limestone has built what buildings?

13. What is the relationship between froth and Benjamin Franklin and froth and Robert Boyle?

14. What are "intuitive sciences"?

15. What intuitive science picked up the study of bubbles?

16. Why do chefs and chemists distrust each other?

17. What men are responsible for bubble science?

18. Helium _____ when excited by electricity.

19. What is the feat of progeny of Genghis Khan?

20. How did William Thomson come to the conclusion that earth was twenty million years old?

21. Lots of _____ inside a rock means that it's _____, while scant traces it's a _____.

22. Rutherford discovered element 104, _____.

23. Zirconium is best known for _____.

24. How do scientist determine the world's oldest rock.

25. Lord Kelvin popularized _____.

26. D'Arcy Wentworth Thompson published what book that was called "the finest work of literature ...."

27. Why did WWI submarine propellers disintegrate and decay?

28. What is sonoluminescence?

29. "Singularity" is usually associated with _____.

30. Why is AIDS a foamy virus?

31. What is the relationship between bubbles and insects and bubbles and peacocks?

32. What makes Diet Coke explode when you drop a Mentos candy?

CHAPTER 18

1. What is the purpose of the standards bureau?

2. What is the BIPM and where is it located?

3. The Kilogram is made of dense _____. What are 3 reasons this is used?

4. Define calibration.

5. Why is flying K20 to Paris an absolute hassle?

6. Where are copies of the Kilogram kept?

7. What does science owe much of its progress to since 1600?

8. The Copernican principle is also called _____.

9. The kilogram is one of seven _____ of measurement.

10. Measurement scientists have redefined a meter a_____ in _____ of a second.

11. What is a "leap" second?

12. Explain how atomic clocks run.

13. Why was cesium convenient as the mainspring for atomic clocks?

14. How fast is a cesium electron?

15. Cesium may be a fine element but it lacks the _____.

16. The best-known dimensionless constant is

17. _____, who during a solar eclipse in 1919 provided the first experimental proof of _____, grew fascinated with _____.

18. Today alpha makes the periodic table possible. How?

19. _____ scrutinized a bizarre site in _____ called _____ and declared that alpha was getting _____.

20. Oklo was powered by nothing but _____, _____, and _____.

21. For a chain reaction to occur, neutrons must not only strike uranium nuclei, they must _____.

22. Star systems are called _____ and _____.

23. Quasars are _____ _____ that tear apart and _____ other stars.

24. Enrico Fermi died of _____ after some brash experiments and won _____ for discovering _____ he really didn't discover.

25. What assignment did Fermi ask his students to perform?

26. What is the Drake Equation?

27. Why is the Drake Equation important?

28. If scientists were looking for life on another planet, what element might they search for?

29. Almost all life forms use _____ _____ in trace amounts. Animals primarily use the _____ in _____.

30. _____ is probably the most important organic chemical on earth because it drives _____ by converting _____ energy into sugars, the basis of the food chain.

31. Magnesium in animals helps _____ function properly.

32. Magnesium on planets implies the presence of _____. How does magnesium help maintain a liquid ocean?

33. Einstein determined that space and time are _____.

34. Discovering life on other planets would be proof the human beings

CHAPTER 19

1. Using context clues from the first paragraph define conundrum.

2. _____ of the particles in the universe are _____, and the other _____ are _____.

3. _____ is the scarcest natural element. What metaphor is used to describe this scarcity?

4. How does astatine still exist if its radioactivity has disintegrated?

5. What is astatine good for?

6. Astatine remains the only element whose discovery was confirmed by a _____.

7. _____ is more stable than either astatine or francium.

8. Attempts to reach the oasis of _____ have made up one of the most exciting fields of physics.

9. To get truly stable, doubly magic elements, they need to figure out ways to add more _____ to their targets.

10. Why is francium more abundant and astatine?

11. The binomial species system in biology is gradually being replaced by _____.

12. Einstein actually won his Nobel Prize for _____

13. What is the "theory of everything"?

14. Richard Feynman called _____ one of the great damn mysteries of the universe.

15. What did Glenn Seaborg and his colleagues accomplish?

16. What are superatoms?

17. What is jellium?

18. A quantum dot is _____.
    An example of a quantum dot is _____.

19. Explain in detail Devils Tower.

20. Who does our author want to donate $1,000 to?

CHAPTER 1
Pgs 23-31

1. Why was antimony great for building custom acids?

    A. Because of antimony's ability to hoard electron-greedy elements around it, it was able to build custom acids.

2. Why couldn't you pick up a substance with a pH of -31?

    A. It would dissolve your hand.

3. What is carborane good for?

    A. It can add an octane kick to gasoline, for one thing, and help make vitamins digestible.

4. Lewis's work was passed over for **the Manhattan Project during WWII.**

5. What possibilities could have contributed to Lewis's death?

    A. Contributors to death may have included 20+ cigars per day for 40+ years, cyanide gas, result of an unfortunate lunch with a young scientific rival.

6. What elements lie in the "great plains" of the periodic table?

    A. Columns 3 through 12 contain the transition metals.

7. Sodium has **11** electrons; magnesium has **12** electrons.

8. Transition metals appear in columns **3** through 12 of the **4th** through **7th** row.

9. Lanthanides are also called the **rare earths.**

10. Why isn't it possible to find a pure sample of a lanthanide in nature?

 A. Lanthanide's brothers always contaminate it.

11. What makes up 99% of an atom's mass?

 A. The nucleus makes up 99% of an atom's mass.

12. Write a paragraph about the difficulties Maria Goeppert had to become recognized as a scientist.

 A. Answers will vary. Possible answers may include discrimination against women in science receiving a Ph.D.

13. She began work in 1948 on the **nucleus,** the core and essence of an atom. The number of positive **protons,** the **atomic number** determines the atom's identity.

14. The atomic number plus the number of **neutrons** is called the **atomic weight.**

15. Explain the mystery that Goeppert-Mayer discovered.

 A. She suggested that the stability in the nucleus is because the protons and neutrons in the nucleus sit in shells just like electrons.

16. Filling nuclear shells leads to **stability**.

17. She proved that nuclei do have shells and do form what she called **magic** nuclei. The magic happens at atomic numbers **2, 8, 20, 28, 50, 82**, and so on.

18. Why is oxygen in seemingly overabundance?

    A. Oxygen is seemingly overabundant because of its 8 protons and 8 neutrons making it doubly magic and eternally stable.

19. Beautiful shapes are **more perfect** according to Plato.

20. What happened in 1963?

    A. Goeppert-Mayer won the Nobel Prize.

21. Why is reading the periodic table up and down or longitudinal more significant than reading from left to right?

    A. Elements in the same column, latitudinal neighbors, are actually far

CHAPTER 2

1. What does the longest word mean, discovered in what year, and how many letters?

   A. The longest word, 1,184 letters describes an important protein of the first virus ever discovered, in 1892—the tobacco mosaic virus.

2. Describe the most versatile element on the periodic table.

   A. The most versatile element on the periodic table is carbon.

3. Each amino acid contains **oxygen** atoms on one end, a **nitrogen** atom on the other, and a trunk of **carbon** atoms in the middle.

4. What allows carbon to build complex chains and why are the bonds steady and stable?

   A. Carbon must form bonds with other atoms in whatever direction it can.

5. What was the 189,819- letter protein shortened to?

   A. This word was shortened to **titin**.

6. What element has been cited as a carbon-based life in other galaxies?

   A. This is element 14, **silicon**.

7. What is the relationship between silicon and an alien?

8. Transition metals appear in columns **3** through 12 of the **4th** through **7th** row.

9. Lanthanides are also called the **rare earths.**

10. Why isn't it possible to find a pure sample of a lanthanide in nature?

    A.   Lanthanide's brothers always contaminate it.

11. What makes up 99% of an atom's mass?

    A.   The nucleus makes up 99% of an atom's mass.

12. Write a paragraph about the difficulties Maria Goeppert had in becoming recognized as a scientist.

    A.   Answers will vary. Possible answers may include discrimination against women in science receiving a Ph.D.

13. She began work in 1948 on the **nucleus,** the core and essence of an atom. The number of positive **protons,** the **atomic number** determines the atom's identity.

14. The atomic number plus the number of **neutrons** is called the **atomic weight.**

15. Explain the mystery that Goeppert-Mayer discovered.

    A.   She suggested that the stability in the nucleus is because the protons and neutrons in the nucleus sit in shells just like electrons.

16. Filling nuclear shells leads to **stability**.

17. She proved that nuclei do have shells and do form what she called **magic** nuclei. The magic happens at atomic numbers **2, 8, 20, 28, 50, 82**, and so on.

18. Why is oxygen in seemingly overabundance?

    A. Oxygen is seemingly overabundant because of its 8 protons and 8 neutrons making it doubly magic and eternally stable.

19. Beautiful shapes are **more perfect** according to Plato.

20. What happened in 1963?

    A. Goeppert-Mayer won the Nobel Prize.

21. Why is reading the periodic table up and down or longitudinal more significant than reading from left to right?

    A. Elements in the same column, latitudinal neighbors, are actually far more intimately related than horizontal neighbors.

CHAPTER 3

1. Bunsen's first love was **arsenic**.

2. Roman assassins used it **to smear on figs**.

3. What is a cacodyl?

    A. Cacodyls are chemicals whose names are based on the Greek word for stinky.

4. What is the best antidote to arsenic and how does it work?

    A. The best antidote to arsenic poisoning is iron oxide hydrate, a chemical related to rust that lumps onto arsenic in the blood and drags it out.

5. After Bunsen became blind he transferred his interest to **natural explosions**. What did he construct in his lab?

    A. He jury-rigged a faux Old Faithful in his laboratory.

6. What ensured Bunsen scientific immortality?

    A. He invented the spectroscope, which used light to study elements.

7.   If a mysterious substance emits red, yellowish green, baby blue, and indigo blue bands what does it contain?

   A.   It contains hydrogen.

8.   What is Bunsen's second great contribution to the periodic table?

   A.   Bunsen's other great contribution to the periodic table was helping develop a team of intellectuals in science in Heidelberg including Dmitri Mendeleev.

9.   How does the periodic table and "The Odyssey" compare?

   A.   Mendeleev grouped elements into small sets like Homer transformed disconnected Greek myths into the "Odyssey"?

10. How did Mendeleev's mother help with her son's career?

   A.   She physically rode him on the back of a horse from Siberia to Moscow, a 1200-mile trip, so that he could attend an elite university. He was rejected. She then rode him another 400 miles to St. Petersburg, his father's alma mater.

11. Mendeleev and Meyer split what medal?

   A.   Both men split the Davy Medal for discovering the "periodic law."

12. What did Mendeleev have a hard time believing in?

   A.   He refused to believe in the reality of atoms.

13. **Metals** are the most ambiguous and knotty elements to place on the table?

14. Why did Mendeleev mesmerize people?

   A.   People were mesmerized when Mendeleev predicted densities and atomic weights of hidden elements that proved correct.

15. Explain why Dostoevsky and Mendeleev were considered outsized characters?

   A. Dostoevsky through "The Gambler" developed ideas in three weeks to pay a gambling debt while Mendeleev threw together the periodic table to meet a deadline.

16. What did the tsar say about a double standard for Mendeleev?

   A. He allowed Mendeleev to remarry before 7 years because he had only one Mendeleev.

17. How does Mendeleev's work compare to Darwin and Einstein's work?

   A. None of these men did all the work in their respective fields but they did most of it and more elegantly.

18. Who discovered gallium?

   A. Lecoq de Boisbaudran discovered gallium.

19. What characteristics of gallium make it a good practical joke?

   A. Though solid at moderate room temperature, gallium melts at 84 degree F.

20. Using context clues define acrimonious.

   A. Their back -forth discussions turned professional to harsh and bitter confrontation.

21. What makes a great story?

   A. What makes a great story is a climax that is surprising and yet inevitable.

22. What does Einstein say about discovery?

    A. It is theory that decides what we can observe.

23. What were a couple of mistakes Mendeleev made?

    A. Mendeleev predicted there were many elements before hydrogen and swore the sun's halo contained a unique element called coronium.

24. How could Mendeleev have solved his frustration about cerium?

    A. He would have solved his frustration if he has traveled just a few hundred miles west from St. Petersburg to Sweden where cerium was first discovered.

25. Why was Johann Friedrich Botteger treated like Rumplestiltskin?

    A. Botteger was locked up so that he could turn silver coins to gold like Rumplestiltskin was locked up to spin gold.

26. Describe the power of porcelain.

    A. Porcelain was hard enough to resist scratching yet translucent like an eggshell. It was a source of power and wealth.

27. What were the secret ingredients of Chinese porcelain?

    A. The secret ingredients of Chinese porcelain were white clay called kaolin and a feldspar rock that fuses into glass at high temperature. Clay and glaze must be baked together.

28. What is Ytterby?

    A. Ytterby is a feldspar mine a dozen miles from Stockholm, on an island.

29 Bright colors are dead giveaways of **lanthanides**.

30. Scandinavians embraced rationalism en masse. What does this mean?

    A.   Great scientists started popping up all over when Scandinavians embraced rationalism en masse.

31. What elements did Gandolin discover?

    A.   Gandolin discovered yttria while other scientists discovered ytterbium, yttrium, terbium, and erbium, thulium, and gadolinium.

CHAPTER 4

Pgs 65-71

1. Prior to 1939 what was the common view of the origin of elements?

   A. The commonsense view that dominated science for centuries was that they don't come from anywhere,

2. What discovery in 1939 began to dissolve the above theory?

   A. The discovery was the sun and other stars heated themselves by fusing hydrogen together to form helium, a process that releases an outsized amount of energy

3. What is technetium and where does it exist?

   A. Technetium is an extremely unstable element that exists in stars.

4. What is B2FH?

   A. B2FH is a paper published in 1957 to explain the theory of stellar nucleosynthesis.

5. When do things really start shaking?

   A. Things really start shaking when hydrogen burns up.

6. There is an interesting metaphor at the bottom of page 66 that explain the change in star matter. What is the metaphor?

   A. The metaphor is a cow chewing its cud.

7. When stars die what do they create?

   A. When stars die, they create molten masses of carbon known as white dwarfs.

8. B2FH traces various fusion reactions and explains the recipe for producing everything up to iron: it's nothing less than **evolution for elements.**

9. Once iron is spotted in a star, it's safe to assume **the rest of the periodic table up to that point is represented.**

10. Iron is the final **peal of a star's natural life**.

11. According to B2FH where do the heaviest elements, twenty-seven through ninety-two, **cobalt** through **uranium** come from?

12. Explain in a short paragraph how elements develop in a supernova.

   A. Gazillions of particles with so much momentum collide so many times per second that they high jump over the normal energy barriers and fuse onto iron.

13. What happened 4.6 billion years ago?

   A. A supernova sent a sonic boom through a flat cloud of space dust about fifteen billion miles wide, the remains of at least 2 previous stars, swirling and eddy.

14. How were the giant planets like Jupiter formed?

   A. These planets formed when a stellar wind blew lighter elements outward toward the fringes.

15. Why is Uranus misnamed?

    A. It is misnamed because it contains zero grams of the element uranium.

16. What is the Shoemaker-Levy 9 comet?

    A. The Shoemaker-Levy 9 comet collided with Jupiter in 1994, 21 fragments struck home.

17. What effect did the Hale-Bopp comet have on Earth?

    A. Jupiter's gravity bent the Hale-Bopp comet toward Earth and 39 cultists committed suicide because they believed that Jupiter divinely deflected it and that it concealed a UFO that would beam them into a higher spiritual plane.

18. What did scientists hope was at the center of Jupiter's core?

    A. The hope was that Jupiter's core could produce a huge gem.

19. What are contained in the black oceans of Jupiter?

    A. The oceans are black liquid metallic hydrogen.

20. Why do elements have strange lives on Jupiter?

    A. It is a "tweener: not a large planet but a failed star.

21. What is the giant red eye?

    A. The giant red eye is a hurricane three times wider that the earth that hasn't dissipated after centuries of furious storming.

22. What is the basic elemental composition of real stars?

    A. The basic composition of real stars is 90% hydrogen, 10% helium, and traces of other elements, including neon.

23. Why is there an abundance of helium and neon toward the center of Jupiter?

A. Helium and neon fall toward the center of Jupiter because it has no nuclear furnace keeping it from falling in.

CHAPTER 4

Pgs. 72-80

1. What are the solar system's rocky planets?

   A. The solar system's rocky planets are Mercury, Venus, Earth, and Mars.

2. Define coalesce

   A. Coalesce means coming together or uniting.

3. How did healthy deposits of all elements form on the planets?

   A. As elements churned around, atoms began tagging up with their twins and chemical cousins, and after billions of passes, healthy sized deposits of each element formed.

4. What is at the core of each planet?

   A. Iron is at the core of each planet.

5. How do the planets around other stars in our solar system differ from the planets around other stars?

   A. Compared to planets around other stars, our system's four rocky planets have different abundances of each type of element.

6. Each solar system has a unique **chemical signature**.

7. The number below each element on the periodic table indicates its **atomic weight**—the number of **protons** plus the number of **neutrons**.

8. How have scientists deduced the earth was formed?

    A. Scientists analyzed the amount and placement of common and rare elements in the earth's crust and deduced how they could have gotten where they are.

9. Who helped fix the date of the planet through experiments on lead and uranium?

    A. Clair Patterson helped fix the date of the planet through experiments on lead and uranium.

10. What two isotopes does uranium break down?

    A. Uranium breaks down into two types of isotopes, 206 and 207.

11. What would Patterson have to do to go back to the year zero?

    A. If he could figure out how much higher the ratio was now than originally, he could use the data to extrapolate backward to year zero.

12. What are preserved hunks of primordial earth?

    A. Meteors, asteroids, and comets are hunks of primordial earth.

13. Meteors are solid **iron**.

14. Where did Patterson get meteor bits to conduct his experiments?

    A. Patterson got meteor bits from Canyon Diablo in Arizona.

15. Why did Pb, lead ruin Patterson's early attempts to analyze meteors?

   A.   Patterson's early attempts to analyze meteors were ruined because of the ambient lead all around us.

16. How did he treat lead to keep out of his space rocks?

   A.   He had to boil equipment in concentrated sulfuric acid to keep human lead out of his pristine rocks.

17. What about the lead from your hair?

   A.   The lead from your hair would contaminate the whole laboratory simply by walking in.

18. What was the metaphor Patterson used for humanity?

   A.   The metaphor Patterson used for humanity as Peanut's character, Pig-Pen.

19. What is the result of Patterson becoming an activist?

   A.   He's the largest reason future children will never eat lead paint chips and gas stations no longer bother to advertise "unleaded" on their pumps.

20. Venus, Mercury, and Mars were formed simultaneously. What does that mean?

   A.   Simultaneously means that they were formed at the same time.

21. What were Luis and Walter Alvarez's discovery?

   A.   The team discovered iridium.

22. Iridium is a siderophile. What is that and where is it found?

 A. A siderophile is an iron-loving element and as a result most of it is tied up in the earth's molten iron core.

23. Besides dinosaurs what else was destroyed 65 million years ago?

 A. Seventy-five percent of all species and 99% of all living beings died around the same time.

24. When was the asteroid-iridium extinction theory seemed proved?

 A. It seem proved when geologists discovered a crater on a Yucatan Peninsula in Mexico.

25. Did all dinosaurs dies out at the same time? Explain.

 A. Dinosaurs died out over hundreds of thousands of years.

26. What is the chance of an asteroid passing close to the sun hitting our planet?

 A. As asteroid passing close to the sun has only slightly better than one chance in a billion of hitting our planet.

27. What is the theory about the sun and a companion star?

 A. Maybe the sun had a companion star around which the earth circled too slowly for us to notice and whose gravity yanked asteroids toward the earth as it approached us.

28. What is the relationship between Nemesis and rhenium?

 A. If Nemesis really did exist and sling rocks at us then those rocks would have the same ratio of rhenium as those in space.

29. What simile was used to describe critics on the Nemesis theory?

 A. Scientists lined up to volley bullets like redcoats in the Revolutionary War.

30. What is the counter argument against Copernican revolution?

    A.   The counter argument is that the sun is dragged along in the tides of our local spiral galaxy and bobs up like a carousel as it drifts.

31. What is the nearest star and how far is it from earth?

    A.   The nearest star is Alpha Centauri is four light-years away.

32. What is an Oort cloud?

    A.   The Oort cloud is made up of space debris that surrounds our solar system that originated with our supernova birth.

CHAPTER 5

1. We can trace chemical warfare back to **ancient Greece**, which used **smoke**.

2. Define harbinger

    A. Harbinger means forerunner.

3   .The **Hague Convention** of 1899 banned chemical weapons in war.

4. Why did the United States refuse to sign this pact?

    A. The US thought the pact was hypocritical if countries were all too happy to mow down eighteen-year-olds with machine guns, sink warships with torpedoes, and let sailors drown in the dark sea.

5. **Bromine** was secretly chosen as a chemical weapon because it irritates the eyes and nose. This agent was a **lacrimator** so potent it could incapacitate a grown man with hot searing tears.

6. **Fritz Haber** was one of the great minds in the history of chemistry when he figured out how to convert **nitrogen** in air – into an industrial product.

7. The one important thing nitrogen does is **replenish soils**.

8. What are the steps Haber used to capture nitrogen?

   A. Haber heated nitrogen to hundreds of degrees, injected some hydrogen gas, turned up the pressure to hundred of times greater than normal air pressure, added some osmium as a catalyst, and voila: common air transmuted into ammonia, NH, the precursor of all fertilizers.

9. We can thank him for feeding most of the world's **6.7** billion people today.

10. What was the real reason Haber pursued this line of experimentation?

    A. He pursued this to build nitrogen explosives for Germany.

11. These were the types of explosives **Timothy McVeigh** used to blow a hole in an **Oklahoma City courthouse** in **1995**.

12. Like petty **Fausts** who twist scientific innovations into efficient killing devices, Haber's story is darker because he was so **skilled**.

13. How did Germany deal with Haber's Jewish heritage?

    A. They converted him to Lutheranism.

14. How did Germany get by the Hague pact?

    A. The Germans declared the pact had no jurisdiction over shells that delivered shrapnel and gas.

15. Why did Haber change from the use of bromine to chlorine?

    A. Chlorine is more aggressive in attacking other elements for one more electron and because chlorine is smaller—each atom can attack the body's cells more nimbly.

16. How does chlorine gas affect the human body?

    A. Chlorine turns victims' skin yellow, green, and black, and glasses over their eyes with cataracts. They die of drowning from the fluid buildup in their lungs.

17. What is Haber's Rule?

    A. The rule quantified the relationship between gas concentration, exposure time, and death rate—which must have required a depressing amount of data to produce.

18. How did Haber's wife react to Fritz's scientific work?

    A. His wife, Clara, walked into the family garden and shot herself in the chest.

19. What was the irony of Huber's Nobel Prize of 1919?

    A. The irony is that he won his prize for producing ammonia from nitrogen used in fertilizer had not protected the Germans from famine during the war.

20. What happened to Haber when Germany lost the war?

    A. He was charged with being an international war criminal.

21. How did the Nazis treat Haber?

    A. The Nazis exiled Haber for his Jewish roots.

22. **Tungsten** would go on to become the "it" metal of WWII.

23. What are Big Berthas?

    A. Big Berthas were super heavy siege guns that battered soldiers' psyches as brutally as they did the trenches of France and Belgium

24. Why was molybdenum a good addition to steel in weaponry?

    A.   Molybdenum could withstand the excessive heat because it melts 4,750 degrees hotter than iron.

25. How and why did the Japanese learn about this metal recipe?

    A.   A master sword maker in the fourteenth century sprinkled molybdenum into his steel and produced the island's most coveted samurai swords.

26. How did a Germany mining company come to own a molybdenum mine in Colorado and why?

    A.   A mining company based in Frankfurt, Germany with a US branch in New York when learned of the abundance of molybdenum seized Bartlett Mountain.

27. What is the relationship between Otis King and Two-Gun Adams?

    A.   Otis King had the claim on Bartlett Mountain and Two-Gun Adams was hired for protection from claim jumpers.

28. What was the relationship between Metallgesellschaft and American Metal?

    A.   Metallgesellschaft was a large German mining company that had smelters, mines, refineries, and other tentacles all over the world. American Metal was a subsidiary of the German company in New York.

29. W or wolfram stands for **tungsten**.

30. Who supplied the Axis powers with tungsten during the war?

    A.   Neutral Portugal supplied tungsten to the Axis powers.

31. What was the theory behind Antonio Salazar supplying tungsten to both sides?

    A.   The theory was that his country's neutral status allowed him to gouge both sides equally.

32. Once added to steel it made excellent drill bits, saw heads, and **kinetic energy penetrators** that could take down tanks.

33. How did the Nazis pay for the tungsten?

    A.   The Nazi paid for the tungsten with gold seized from the Jews.

34. Explain why the US disagreed with Winston Churchill.

    A.   The US couldn't understand why Churchill agreed with Salazar that it was "quite right" to trade tungsten with the enemy.

35. When did Salazar issue a full tungsten embargo on Germany?

    A.   Portugal issued a full embargo on Germany on June 4, 1944 the day after D-Day.

36. What did Rhett Butler say about the making of fortunes?

    A.   He said fortunes could only be made during the building up or tearing down of an empire.

37. Every metal has a niche:

    Gadolinium: **perfect for magnetic resonance imaging (MRI)**

    Neodymium: **makes powerful lasers**

    Scandium: **additives for baseball bats and bike frames, lightweight helicopters.**

38. Describe the 2 myths that tantalum and niobium were named after.

   A. Niobe bragged about her 7 lovely and 7 handsome sons who were killed by Olympians. Tantalus, Niobe's mother killed his own son and served him at a banquet. Tantalus served eternity standing up to his neck in a river with a branch loaded with apples dangling above his nose.

39. Tantalum and niobium are vital for making **compact cell phones**.

40. Why did supplying coltan cause more problems in the Congo?

   A. People didn't care how and where the coltan came from and how it   affected the people of the Congo.

41. What is one reason the killing of gorillas came about?

   A. Because so many of the farmers were prospecting for coltan, they took to hunting gorillas for meat almost to extinction.

42. Why is tin now a major problem for the Congo?

   A. Tin is now funding the fighting in the Congo killing millions.

43. What did Joseph Conrad say about the Congo?

   A. Regarding the Congo, it is the "vilest scramble for loot that ever disfigured the history of human conscience."

44. More than **5 million** people have died in the Congo since the mid 1990s.

CHAPTER 6

1. Why have some species of elements gone extinct?

    A. Some species of elements have gone extinct because their nuclei, their cores, were too fragile to survive in nature.

2. What simile describes Henry Mosley's dedication to his work?

    A. He treated his lab work like a deathbed vigil, staying for fifteen hour stretches.

3. How did Mosley feel about foreigners at Manchester?

    A. He expressed open disgust at the "scented dirtiness" of foreigners at Manchester.

4. Describe in a sentence or two how X-rays are formed?

    A. Nature abhors a vacuum, other electrons rush into fill the gap, and the crashing about causes them to release high-energy X-rays.

5. What are the seven holes in the table?

    A. The seven holes in the table are elements 43, 61, 72, 85, 87, and 91.

6. Explain the meeting between Georges Urbain and Moseley?

   A. Urbain challenged Moseley questioning his claim in chemistry.

7. What was the "one of the most hideous and most irreparable crimes in history?"

   A. Moseley's death in WWI was considered irreparable because the world lost a great scientist.

8. Explain what, where, and when element sixty-one was discovered.

   A. Scientists from Oak Ridge National Laboratory in Tennessee rose at a scientific meeting in Philadelphia and announced that after shifting through some spent uranium ore; they had discovered element sixty-one, promethium.

9. Who was it named after?

   A. Promethium was named after the Titan in Greek mythology who stole fire, gave it to humankind, and was tortured by having a vulture dine on his liver.

10. What was the famous offspring of plutonium and uranium?

    A. The famous offspring of plutonium and uranium was the atomic bomb.

11. How did Luis Alvarez react to Otto Hahn's experiments on **fission**?

    A. He was so excited he ran from the barbershop and scooped up a Geiger counter and ran to find some irradiated uranium. It was a mad tear.

12. What was the tool devised to understand how subatomic particles behaved?

    A. Quantum mechanics was the tool to understand how subatomic particles behaved.

13. What is the field of radioactivity?

    A. The field of radioactivity is the study of how nuclei fall apart.

14. What is the most powerful atomic "shrapnel"?

    A. Gamma decay is the simplest and most deadly shrapnel.

15. Explain Alpha decay and Beta decay.

    A. Beta decay was understood as the conversion of neutrons to protons or vice versa—and it's because the proton number changes that beta decay converts an atom into a different element. Alpha decay also converts elements and is the most dramatic change on a nuclear level—two neutrons and two protons are shorn away.

16. What did Leo Szilard patent?

    A. He patented a cascade known as a chain reaction.

17. Why did a few undiscovered elements remain undiscovered?

    A. They remain undiscovered because they were intrinsically unstable.

18. What strategy did the Manhattan Project adopt?

    A. The Manhattan Project adopted the Monte Carlo method.

19. Why was it important to know how much plutonium and uranium was needed to make a bomb?

    A. Too little and the bomb would fizzle out. Too much and the bomb would blow up just fine, but the cost of prolonging the war by months.

20. What was meant by "building bombs numerically?" What were the "computers?"

    A. Numerically meant neutron-by-neutron, nanosecond-by-nanosecond. Female employees who crunched long tables of data.

21. The Ulam -and –von- Neumann form of probability of numbers was eventually called the **plug and chug.**

22. What are "supers"?

    A. Supers are multistage devices a thousand times more powerful than standard A-bombs.

23. What is a cobalt-60 dirty bomb and what kinds of damage can it do?

    A. Dirty bombs kill with gamma radiation—malignant X-rays, which result from frantic radioactive events, and in addition to burning people frightfully, they dig down into the bone marrow and scramble the chromosomes in white blood cells.

24. Explain the difference in radiation in the nuclear bomb and the dirty bomb.

    A. All nuclear bombs release some radiation, but with dirty bombs, radiation is the whole point.

25. What are the long- term effects of Cobalt 60 in the earth?

    A. Cobalt 60 atoms settle into the ground like tiny land mines. Enough would go off right away to make it necessary to flee, but after five years fully half of the cobalt would still be armed.

26. How long would it take for the land to recover?

    A. It would take a whole lifetime for the land to recover.

27. What was the theme of the movie, "Dr. Strangelove"?

    A. The movie shows the insanity of nuclear war.

28. What is MAD?

    A. MAD mean mutual assured destruction—the idea that both sides would lose in a nuclear war.

29. What happened between the Soviet Union and the United States at the end of this chapter?

    A. Tensions turned into the cold war—a struggle that so infiltrated our society that not even the pristine periodic table escaped its stain.

CHAPTER 7

1. What were scientists doing in the laboratories that ended in being a "bitter creation?"

    A. At this time the naming of element would soon become a new theater for the cold war.

2. What was the element created by Edwin McMillan?

    A. McMillan created neptunium.

3. How were scientists used during WWII?

    A. Scientists worked on military projects such as radar.

4. What circumstances led Seaborg to conduct science that discovered the element with a +7 charge named **plutonium**.

5. What was the relationship between Glenn Seaborg and Al Ghiorso?

    A. Although they were opposites in looks, personality, and temperament, they hit it off.

6. What job did Seaborg give Ghiorso?

    A. Seaborg put Ghiorso to work—wiring detectors.

7. What metaphor does the author use to describe the success of discovering elements by Ghiorso and Seaborg?

    A. They used the biggest guns as the big-game hunters of science.

8. What are alpha particles? What are their advantages over neutrons?

    A. Alpha particles are clusters of two protons and two neutrons that are easier to accelerate to high speeds than mulish neutrons.

9. What happened when alphas struck plutonium?

    A. When alphas struck the plutonium, the Berkeley team got two new elements at a stroke, since element 96 decayed into element 95 by ejecting a proton.

10. The 2 new elements were named **americium** and **curium**.

11. Why did Ghiorso want to give chemical symbol Bm to berkelium?

    A. The wanted to call berkelium Bm because it was such a stinker to discover.

12. What was element 99 and 100 and where were they discovered?

    A. The team discovered elements 99 and 100 einsteinium and fermium, in radioactive coral after a hydrogen bomb test in the Pacific in 1952.

13. Why was there disagreement in naming element 101 mendelevium?

    A. Diplomatically, it was daring to honor a Russian scientist during the cold war, and it was not a popular choice domestically.

14. What were element 102 and 103, their names and who they were named after?

    A. Element 102, nobelium was named after Alfred Nobel, dyna-mite inventor and founder of the Nobel Prizes, and element 103, lawrencium, was named after Berkeley Radiation Labo-ratory founder and director Ernest Lawrence in the early 1960s.

15. What two elements were discovered in Russia?

    A. Ruthenium and samarium were discovered in Russia.

16. What were the reasons that Russia never had the scientific genius as others had?

    A. Because of despotic tsars, an agrarian economy, poor schools, and harsh weather Russia never fostered the scientific genius it might have.

17. Explain the October Revolution that occurred in November.

    A. Because Russia used the misaligned Julius Caesar calendar instead of the modern Gregorian calendar it was weeks behind and explains the lag time for the October Revolution occurring in November.

18. How was fluorine a benefit to public health? What did the John Birch Society think about this?

    A. The John Birch Society thought the addition of fluorine to tap water was some sort of communist conspiracy even though the addition has allowed people to die with their own teeth for the first time in history.

19. What did Lysenko falsely claim under Russia's Stalin?

    A. Lysenko denounced the regressive idea that living things, including crops, inherit traits and genes from their parents.

20. How did Stalin treat scientists?

   A. Stalin forced scientists to work in state slave labor camps, prison, and nickel mines.

21. What is black snow?

   A. It snowed black due to the arsenic, lead, and cadmium pollution from the mines.

22. Why were physicists left in peace under Stalin?

   A. Because physics overlaps with weapons research physicists escaped the worst punishment.

23. What happened to the 650 scientists of the elite Academy of Sciences?

   A. These scientists were rounded up in one purge of science elite, many being shot for opposing progress.

24. How was Flyorov able to gain his own lab under Stalin?

   A. He sent letters playing into politics so that he could continue his research.

25. What is "blackboard science"?

   A. Blackboard sciences were esoteric topics too hard to explain to laypeople and unlikely to ruffle narrow-minded ideologues.

26. What is IUPAC what did it arbitrate?

   A. IUPAC, International Union of Pure and Applied Chemistry, was needed to arbitrate the naming of elements, argued by the Soviets and the US.

27. What are elements 104 to 109?

    A. 104 rutherfordium, 105 dubnium, 107 bohrium, 108 hassium, 109 meitnerium.

28. Victor Ninov caused controversy. Why?

    A. Berkeley lured Bulgarian Victor Ninov away from the Germans to renew their science program. But they brought shame on the program when he inserted false positives into his data files and passed them off as real.

CHAPTER 8

1. Who was the greatest element craftsman of an earlier era who nabbed the most slippery and elusive element on the entire table?

   A.   Emilio Segre was coined the greatest element craftsman by the Time magazine in 1960.

2. What was Segre's nationality?

   A.   He was a Jewish immigrant.

3. Segre wrote Pauling for advice on experiments with **radioactive beryllium.**

4. **Vulcanized rubber, Teflon,** and **penicillin** were all mistakes.

5. Serendipitous clumsiness and outright blunders have pushed science ahead all through history. What does serendipitous mean?

   A.   Serendipitous means when good things happen accidentally.

6. No element has been discovered for the "first time" more times than **element 43.**

7. What element did Masataka Ogawa isolate that was reexamined in 2004?

   A.   Ogawa isolated element 75, rhenium.

8. Why had a continent-wide plot rose to discredit the Germans?

 A. Because nationalism had destroyed Europe, they did not look kindly on German names.

9. Why had element 43 proved so elusive?

 A. Element 43 proved elusive because every atom of it in the earth's crust had disintegrated radioactively into molybdenum millions of years ago.

10. Ernest Lawrence invented an atom smasher called a **cyclotron**.

11. Segre heard that the cyclotron used replaceable **molybdenum** parts.

12. Describe Walter Noddack's visit with Segre.

 A. Noddack visited Segre wearing full Nazi uniform dress including swastikas.

13. Lawrence was obtuse with people. What does obtuse mean?

 A. Obtuse means slow to understand.

14. What consequential discovery did Enrico Fermi miss?

 A. He had induced uranium fission years before anyone else but didn't realize it.

15. Segre later became a **science historian** as well as a hunter of **wild mushrooms**.

16. Who were the women who clearly discovered fission?

 A. Ida Noddack, Irene Joliot-Curie, and Lise Meitner help discover fission.

17. What was nature's first forbidden element?

    A. Neptunium was the first forbidden element.

18. During 1925 **Germany** was the center of the scientific universe.

19. Pauling proved to be the **Leonardo** of chemistry. Whom is this referring? **Leonardo de Vinci got details down right the first time.**

20. Pauling proved "that chemistry could be **understood** rather than being **memorized**"

21. Why are snowflakes six sided?

    A. Snowflakes are six sided because of the hexagonal structure of ice.

22. Why does sickle-cell anemia kill people?

A. Sickle-cell anemia kills people because the misshaped hemoglobin in their red blood cells cannot hold on to oxygen.

23. Pauling also showed how proteins could form long cylinders called **alpha helixes**.

24. The study of **atomic ecosystems** was a step up in sophistication from creating new elements.

25. Explain the discovery of DNA in 1869.

    A. Friedrich Miescher poured alcohol and the stomach juice of pigs onto pus-soaked bandages until a sticky grey substance remained and declared deoxyribonucleic acid or DNA

26. Linus Pauling's son, Peter, worked in the same lab as James Watson and **Francis Crick**.

27. **X-ray crystallography** shows the shapes of molecules.

28. **Antiprotons** are the mirror image of regular protons: have a negative charge, may travel backward in time, and scarily, will annihilate any "real" matter such as you and me, on contact.

CHAPTER 9

After reading chapter 9 add details to each topic.

Kamioka mines

> A mine in central Japan began digging up gold, lead, silver, and copper in 710 AD. Twelve hundred years later miners began processing cadmium. Deep penetrating bone pain developing in farmers around the mine.

Itai-itai

> A Japanese word that means suffering. Also called the ouch, ouch disease.

Norboru Hagen

> Hagen, a doctor, produced an epidemiological map plotting cases of itai-itai. He also created a hydrological map showing where the Jinzu River deposited its runoff. Went public with the results in 1961.

Godzilla

> Because Japan retained the stigma brought on by cadmium poisoning, it was cadmium tipped missiles that killed Godzilla in "The Return of Godzilla".

Big Four Pollution Diseases

> Mass industrial poisoning from itai-itai, twice with mercury, once with sulfur dioxide and nitrogen dioxide.

Mimic

> Whereas most elements act like themselves, thallium can mimic or act like many elements into many different biochemical niches. That is why thallium is considered the deadliest element on the table.

Graham Frederick Young

> A serial killer began experimenting on his family by sprinkling thallium into their teacups and stew pots. Known as the poisoner's poison. Thallium has killed spies, orphans, and great-aunts with large estates.

Fidel Castro

> A CIA plan to powder Fidel Castro's socks with a talcum powder tainted with thallium which would cause his hair and beard to fall out never came to pass.

Knick-knack

> Knick-knacks or desk -top ornaments are made out of bismuth can form hopper crystals, which twist themselves into elaborate rainbow staircases. Bismuth has widespread use in paints and dyes. Bismuth expands when it freezes.

Half- life

> Half-life is the amount of time it would take 50% of the sample to disintegrate. It is a common measurement of radioactive elements.

Medicinal

Although bismuth shares a column with arsenic and antimony, it is actually benign. Doctors prescribe it to sooth ulcers, and it the "bis" in hot-pink Pepto-Bismol. It is probably the most misplaced element on the table.

Noble metal

Instead of labeling bismuth a freakish anomaly, you might consider it a noble metal.

David Hahn

As a sixteen year old from Detroit and an Eagle Scout, he erected a nuclear reactor in a potting shed in his mother's backyard. Disasters began to happen. He learned about the three main nuclear processes—fusion, fission, and radioactive decay.

Breeder reaction

David Hahn began building a breeder reactor, which makes its own fuel through a clever combination of radioactive species.

CHAPTER 10

After reading chapter 10 add details to each topic.

Obscure (not well known) elements

> Obscure elements do obscure things inside the body, often bad, sometimes good. An element toxic in one circumstance can be a lifesaving drug in another, and elements that get metabolized in unexpected ways can provide new diagnostic tools in doctors' clinics.

Antiseptic powers

> Both copper and silver have antiseptic powers.

Copper

> Copper has proved to be the simplest, cheapest way to improve infrastructure because when bacteria, fungi, or algae inch across something made of copper, they absorb copper atoms, which disrupt their metabolism. The microbes choke and die after a few hour.

Oligodynamic

Oligodynamic or self-sterilizing effect makes metals more sterile than wood or plastic and explains why we have brass doorknobs and metal railings in public places. It also explains why most well handled coins of the US realm contain close to 90% copper or are copper coated.

Vanadium

Vanadium is the best spermicide ever devised. It is not on the market because knowing it has desirable effects in test tubes is much different from knowing how to harness those effects to create a safe medicine.

Mt. Fuji

Despite its mild toxicity, vanadium water from the springs of Mt. Fuji is sold online as a cure for diabetes because it lowers blood glucose levels.

Gadolinium

Gadolinium is a potential cancer assassin because its value springs from its abundance of unpaired electron.

MRI-Tumors

Because non-canceling electrons allows gadolinium to be magnetized more strongly than any other element—a nice feature for magnetic resonance imaging (MRI). Highly magnetic bits like gadolinium take longer to relax, the MRI machine picks up on that difference-enabling doctors to pick tumors out on an MRI scan more easily.

Side effects

It causes kidney problems in some patients who cannot flush it out of their systems, and other report that it causes their muscles to stiffen up like early stages of rigor mortis and their skin to harden like a hide, making breathing difficult in some cases.

Silver

> Silver has the same self-sterilizing effects as copper. The difference between silver and copper is that silver, if ingested, colors the skin blue, permanently.

The Blue Man

> A condition called argyria isn't fatal and causes no internal damage. The Blue Man had ingested an overdose of silver nitrate to cure his syphilis.

Stan Jones-Y2K

> Stan Jones was a candidate for the US Senate in 2001 despite being startling blue. He became obsessed with the Y2K computer crash in 1995 so he began distilling a heavy-metal moonshine in his backyard by dipping silver wires attached to 9-volt batteries into tubs of water, He drank his stash faithfully for 4 years until January 2000.

Handedness

> Louis Pasteur discovered the property of biomolecules called handedness, which is the very essence of living matter. Every amino acid in every protein in your body has a left-handed twist to it. Every life form that has ever existed is exclusively left-handed.

Tartaric acid-Louis Pasteur

> Tartaric acid is a harmless waste product of wine production composed of decomposed grape seeds and yeast carcasses and collects as crystals in the dregs of wine kegs. He showed that life has a strong bias for molecules of only one handedness, or "chirality."

Gerhard Domagk-prontosil

> When Domagk's daughter's system became infected with a broken needle in her arm, the father took a long shot and used a new red industrial dye, prontosil to cure her.

IGF-FDR-Sulfonamide

IGF, I. G. Farbenindustrie, who Domagk worked for, filed for patent extension instead of Domagk himself. The drug, protosil, saved the life of FDR, Franklin Delano Roosevelt Jr. It wasn't prontosil that fought off bacteria, but a derivative of it, sulfonamide, which mammal cells produce by splitting prontosil in two.

Hitler

Hitler hated the Nobel committee for awarding the 1935 Nobel Peace Prize to an anti-Nazi journalist and pacifist, so the Der Fuhrer had made it basically illegal for any German to win a Nobel Prize. Domagk was brutalized for his crime, but his drugs saved Winston Churchill.

Chiral chemicals

Chirality was the sole "well-marked line of demarcation that at the present can be drawn between the chemistry of dead matter and the chemistry of living matter.

Thalidomide

The curative of the active ingredient was mixed in with the wrong- handed form because the scientists couldn't separate them. The freakish birth defects that followed—especially children born without legs or arms, their hands or feet stitched like turtle flippers to their trunks—made thalidomide the most notorious pharmaceutical of the twentieth century.

William Knowles

A St. Louis chemist, William Knowles began playing around with an unlikely elemental hero, rhodium, to prove that dead matter if you were clever about it could invigorate living matter.

Catalysts

Catalysts speed up chemical reactions.

Oliver Sacks—L-dopa—Awakenings—Volcano metaphor

Oliver Sack's book <u>Awakenings</u> shows how L-dopa given to Parkinson's patients in a catatonic state erupted to life.

CHAPTER 11

After reading chapter 11 add details to each topic.

<u>Handbook of Chemistry and Physics</u>

    2,804 page <u>Handbook of Chemistry and Physics</u> lists every physical property of every element to far more decimal places than you'd ever need.

Space shuttle Columbia

    The most advanced space shuttle ever designed—set to launch on its first mission in April when technicians crawled into the compartment for a routine systems check they slumped over.

Apollo 1

    3 astronauts burned to death during training

Pure oxygen

    Was allowed to circulate in spacecraft, not air that contains 80% nitrogen. In pure oxygen flames will burn faster and hotter without the dilution of atmospheric nitrogen to absorb some of the heat or otherwise interfere.

Inert nitrogen

NASA decided to use inert gases (nitrogen) instead of pure oxygen.

John Bjornstad , Forest Cole

Both technicians died of nitrogen poisoning on the Columbia mission.

Kills with kindness

Because nitrogen is odorless and colorless and causes no acid buildup in our veins, we breathe it in and out easily, so our lungs feel relaxed and it snags no mental trip wires.

Per-Ingvar Branemark, femurs of rabbits, titanium, prosthetics

Per-Ingvar Branemark was studying how bone marrow produces new blood cells by chiseling out holes in the femurs of rabbits and covered the holes with an eggshell-thin titanium window. What he found was that the titanium locked like a vice onto the femur. This revolutionized the field of prosthetics.

Osteoblasts

Titanium hypnotized blood cells: it triggers zero immune response and even cons the body's osteoblasts, its bone-forming cells, into attaching themselves to it as if there was no difference between element twenty-two and actual bone.

Collagen

The body attacks plastic shards and the tissue around them, covering them with collagen.

Touch, taste, smell

Our sensory equipment bridges physical bodies and our incorporate minds. The deception of titanium is an exception

Tellurium

If someone spills the tiniest bit of tellurium on himself, he will reek like pungent garlic for weeks.

Beryllium

Beryllium, element four, tastes like sugar. Although funny in small doses, it quickly becomes toxic.

Miraculin

This protein strips out the unpleasant sourness in foods without altering the overtones of their taste, so that apple cider vinegar tastes like apple cider, or Tabasco sauce like marinara. It does this both by muting the taste buds for sour and by bonding to the taste buds.

Sour

Sour simply is what we taste when our taste buds open up and hydrogen ions rush in.

Gymnema sylvestre

A chemical in the leaves of the plant Gymnema sylvestre will neuter miraculin, the miracle protein that turns sour into sweet.

Reversals

There are 4 pair of reversals among the ninety-two natural elements—argon-potassium, cobalt—nickel, iodine—tellurium, thorium—protactinium.

Gandhi, iodine, Salt March to Dandi

In 1930 Gandhi led the Indian people in the famous Salt March to Dandi, to protest the oppressive British salt tax. This was something the Indians could produce on their own but it had no iodine. Adding iodine to the salt was the most effective way to prevent birth defects and mental retardation. But Gandhi saw this as one more step to colonialism.

Hypochondriacs, iodized salt, government

Because the government banned common salt, some hypochondriacs worried that iodized salt would spread cancer, diabetes, and tuberculosis.

Goiter, thyroid, hormones

A lack of trace iodine causes goiter, an ugly swelling of the thyroid gland in the neck. If the deficiency persists, the thyroid gland shrivels up. Since the thyroid regulates the production and release of hormones, including brain hormones, the body cannot run smoothly without it.

Bertrand Russell, chemistry through and through

Bertrand Russell, a pacifist, said, "For instance, a deficiency of iodine will turn a clever man into an idiot." There is no way to separate the soul from the body and chemistry is through and through

CHAPTER 12

1. No less than a scientific history, there's a **social history** of the elements.

2. Why is Poland compared to a cheap theater set or a country on wheels?

   A. This is because of all the exits and entrances on the world stage.

3. What were some obstacles standing in the way of Marie Sklodowska's scientific education?

   A. Tsarist Russia had backward views on educating women and she agitated against the wrong people politically.

4. Marie's work on **uranium,** the heaviest natural metal provided a crucial insight: **its chemistry was separate from its physics.**

5. What was the species whose population exploded during the twentieth century?

   A. The species was the refugee scientist.

6. Why was Curie studying pitchblende?

   A. Pitchblende was a uranium waste product, 300 times more radioactive as pure uranium, stirred in a cauldron with "an iron rod almost as big as myself."

7. What was the element named that Marie Curie discovered. Why was it named this?

   A. Marie Curie first isolated polonium—from the Latin for Poland, Polonia—after her nonexistent homeland.

8. What was the scandal caused by Curie and Paul Langevin? How did it end?

   A. Paul Langevin, Marie Curie's scientific colleague, was also her lover, which caused a scandal after a conference in Brussels. It ended with Langevin fighting pistol duels to salvage Curie's honor, though no one was shot. However, Mrs. Langevin knocked out Paul with a chair.

9. Curie had a **femme fatale** reputation. What is this?

   A. A femme fatale is a mysterious and seductive woman whose charms ensnare her lovers in bonds of irresistible desire.

10. Why could polonium be a mocking metaphor for Poland?

    A. Because polonium decays so quickly it could be a mocking metaphor for Poland.

11. Describe a Radithor?

    A. Radithor is a company that sold individual pre-seeped bottles of radium and thorium for medicinal uses.

12. What happened to Alexander Litvinenko?

    A. Litvinenko was an ex-KGB spy who ate polonium-laced sushi and appeared in videos looking like a teenage leukemia victim, having lost all his hair, even his eyebrows, his former Kremlin employers became the prime suspects.

13. What was considered Irene Joliot-Curie and Frederic Joliot-Curie work?

  A. They figured out a method for converting tame elements into artificially radioactive atoms by bombarding them with subatomic particles.

14. Why was the death of Irene Curie ironic?

  A. Irene Curie's death as well as her mother's proved ironic because the cheap radioactive substances she made possible have since become crucial medical tools

15. How did Hevesy waste 2 years of time?

  A. Radium-D was radioactive lead and therefore could not be separated chemically. Hevesy wasted two years of his life trying to tease lead and radium-D apart before giving up.

16. How does the Geiger counter and Hevasy's dinner relate?

  A. In order to prove that his landlady was recycling meat day in and day out, he sprinkled lead on it the then used a Geiger counter on it to prove his point.

17. Who was Niels Bohr?

  A. Hevasy studied with Niels Bohr, a major quantum physicist, in Copenhagen.

18. What started as a scientific argument and became a political dispute about territory and boundaries? To what is this referring?

  A. Philosophers of science also leapt on the story to proclaim that Mendeleevian chemistry was dead and Bohrian physics ruled the realm.

19. What does "stinks of Huns" have to do with a Nobel Prize?

    A. The French considered Bohr and Hevesy Germans even though they were Danish and Hungarian respectively and because of this their discoveries were not trusted.

20. Describe the dire problems Hevesy faced besides his Nobel Prize.

    A. Because of his Jewish ancestry, Hevesy left Germany for Copenhagen.

21. How did Hitler overlook the gold medals?

    A. Hevesy dissolved medals with a caustic mix of nitric and hydrochloric acids, which left an orange aqua mixture. After V-E Day, the medals were later recast.

22. Why was "brevium" changed to "protactinium"?

    A. Because the atoms of brevium live hundreds of thousands of years, they rechristened it protactinium or "parent of actinium".

23. Who discovered element 91?

    A. Although Kazimierz Fajans detected the short-lived atoms of element 91, (brevium), Meitner and Hahn sometimes receive credit for co-discovering element ninety-one today.

24. Why was Meitner smitten with Hahn?

    A. Hahn recognized her worth and chose to work alongside her, where he performed the chemistry and she performed the physics.

25. What did Hitler do in 1933?

    A. Hitler ran all the Jewish scientists out of the country in 1933—causing the first major wave of refugee scientists.

26. Why did Meitner's world collapse?

    A. Because Hitler embraced only Aryan Austrians, anyone remotely Jewish was in trouble. She was forced to flee to Sweden where she accepted a job a one of the Nobel science institutes.

27. Why didn't Hahn receive the Nobel Prize in 1943?

    A. Even though Hahn deserved the prize, the Nobel committee decided to reward nuclear fission with a prize.

28. Should Hahn have received the Nobel Prize in 1944 alone? Explain your answer.

    Answers will vary.

29. Element **109** is now and forever will be known as **meitnerium**.

30. Who was this named after?

    A. Lise Meitner

CHAPTER 13

Pgs. 223-228

1. The history of money is tangled with the history of **counterfeiting**.

2 .Throughout history what have passed for currency?

   A. Cattle, spices, porpoise teeth, salt, cocoa beans, cigarettes, beetle legs, and tulips have all passed for currency.

3 .Describe the myth called Midas.

   A. Midas asked that whatever he touched turned to gold.

4. Describe the kingdom of the real Midas.

   A. The Bonze Age began in Midas's neighborhood around 3000 BC. Casting bronze, an alloy of tin and copper, was the high-tech field of the day, and although the metal remained expensive, the technology had penetrated most kingdoms by the time of his reign.

5. Bronze metals differ depending on the percentages of **tin, copper,** and other elements where the metals were mined.

6. Zinc mixed with copper forms **brass.**

7. Describe the difference in look of brass and bronze.

    A. The shine of brass is more alluring, subtler, and little more golden. Bronze is shiny but with overtones of copper.

8. Brass was passed as **gold** in Midas's kingdom.

9. What is the difference between the dream of finding gold and a real gold rush?

    A. The desire for a great adventure and the love of riches are practically built into human nature. However, gold rushes were awful, dirty, dangerous affairs, with bears and lice and mine collapses and lots of pathetic whoring and gambling.

10. What is fool's gold?

    A. Iron pyrite is faux gold.

11. Discribe the gold rush of the Outback.

    A. In 1893 when one of the horses lost a shoe twenty miles from home and they broke down, they collected eight pounds of gold nuggets just walking around.

12. Describe tellurides.

    A. Tellurium combines with gold to form some garish-sounding minerals—krennerite, petzite, sylvnite, and calaverite with varying color, one of them yellow.

13. Some tellurium compounds smell pungent, **like garlic magnified a thousand times.**

14. Why did "hell finally break loose"?

    A. Hell finally broke loose on May 29, 1896 when calaverite used to build Hannan's Find contained five hundred ounces of gold per ton of rock.

15. Relate Kalgoorlie and the Golden Mile.

    A. Hannan's Find was soon renamed Kalgoorlie, became the world's largest gold producer and called it the Golden Mile.

16. The first real money, coins made of a **natural silver-gold alloy called electrum** in **Lydia**. King **Croesus** figured out how to separate **electrum** into silver and gold coins, establishing a **real currency system.**

17. Describe the counterfeiting of King Polycrates.

    A. King Polycrates began buying off his enemies in Sparta with lead slugs plated with gold.

18. Today, counterfeiting is considered **a straight case of fraud** but for most of history it was considered **precious metal currency**. Convicts could **hang**.

19. The basic economic law is

    A. The basic economic law is that you can make far more money plying an honest trade than spending hundreds of hours making "free"

CHAPTER 13 CONTINUED
229-237

1. What was Newton employment at the end of the 1600s?

   A.   Newton became master of the Royal Mint of England.

2. Endemic means common in a particular place. What form of counterfeiting was endemic in seedier parts of London?

   A.   Clipping coins by shaving the edges and melting the scrapes together to make new coins was endemic to London.

3. How did William Chaloner pay for his crime of counterfeiting?

   A.   William Chaloner was hanged and publicly disemboweled.

4. What were the advantages of paper money over coins?

   A.   The ores for making coins were expensive, coins themselves were cumbersome, and the wealth based on them depended too much on unevenly distributed mineral resources. Coins were also easier for most people to counterfeit.

5. Why is the situation vice versa these days?

   A.   Nowadays anyone with a laser printer can make a decent $20 bill.

6. Metals like **europium** help governments combat swindling.

7. What determines the colors of light?

    A. The colors of light depend on the relative heights of the starting and ending energy levels.

8. What is the difference between normal emissions of light and florescence?

    A. Formal emissions of light involve just electrons, but fluorescence involves whole molecules.

9. How does the EU help prevent counterfeiting?

    A. Counterfeiting is difficult because the European Union uses an eponymous element in the ink on its paper bills.

10. Why is that (color) shift useful?

    A. The fluorescing dyes are selected so that europium appears dull under visible light, and a counterfeiter might be lulled into thinking he has a perfect replica.

11. Explain why there are two euros in each banknote.

    A. There is one we see day to day and a second, hidden euro mapped directly onto the first—an embedded code.

12. Describe Primo Levi's currency and how it was used?

    A. While working in a prison chemical plant, Levi began making small sticks of cerium, making it an ideal flint for cigarette lighters that he trades to the civilian workers in exchange for bread and soup.

13. How was <u>The Wonderful Wizard of Oz</u> an allegory?

    A. It was perhaps an allegory about the relative merits of the silver versus the gold standard.

14. Ounce-by-ounce, the most valuable element, among elements you can actually buy is **rhodium**.

15. How did Paul McCartney celebrate becoming the bestselling musician of all time?

    A.   He celebrated with a disk made of rhodium.

16. Why did aluminum cap the Washington Monument?

    A.   The aluminum cap was used to show off the country's industrial prowess.

17. Who was the "aluminum boy wonder"?

    A.   Charles Hall was the aluminum boy wonder.

18. What was one of the most successful business ventures in history?

    A.   Alcoa was one of the most successful business ventures in history.

19. How rich was Hall when he died in 1914?

    A.   When he died in 1914 he was worth $650 million.

20. Money **talks.**

CHAPTER 14

1. As science became more sophisticated what dictated when, if, and how science got done?

    A. Big money dictated when, if, and how science got done.

2. Why were the rich exploring sciences?

    A. No one else had the leisure to sit around and argue about what some obscure rocks were made of.

3. Why based on the above answer were the elements named like they were?

    A. Gentlemen throughout Europe received educations heavy in the classics, and many element names—cerium, thorium, promethium—point to ancient myths.

4. Who was considered by many to be the most accomplished German ever to live?

    A. Johann Wolfgang von Goethe was considered by many to be the most accomplished German ever to live.

5. Explain the imagery of a Quasimodo-like job.

    A. Quasimodo-like job refers to working in a dungeon-like basement with someone who had shoulder-length, tendriled hair, and his big arms and chest would have seemed bulking had he stood taller than five feet six.

6. Using context clues what does epochal mean?

    A. Epochal means world changing.

7. Define <u>dilettante.</u>

    A. Dilettante means someone who dabbles in science or art in a superficial way.

8. Goethe's novel <u>Elective Affinities </u>was written as a metaphor **for marriages working like chemical reactions.**

9. What is the difference between Neptunists and Plutonists?

    A. Neptunists thought rocks precipitated from minerals in the ocean while Putonists argued that volcanoes and heat deep within the earth form most rocks

10. Why would Goethe be crushed today?

    A. He would be crushed to learn that its science and philosophy would soon disintegrate and that people now read his work strictly for its literary value.

11. What were some differences between Goethe and J. W. Dobereiner?

    A. Dobereiner was a provincial man with no chemistry degree and a poor resume while Goethe was a gentleman with a good education.

12. What element is Dobereiner associated with?

    A.   Dobereiner is associated with element strontium.

13. What are triads? Give 2 examples.

    A.   Triads are groups of 3 elements with linking characteristics: chlorine, bromine, and iodine; sulfur, selenium, and tellurium.

14. What are the Dobereiner's pillars?

    A.   Dobereiner's pillars are recognized as columns to the periodic table.

15. What made Dobereiner famous?

    A.   He invented the first portable lighter.

16. "The history of science is **science itself**."

17. How does the periodic table according to Goethe resemble art?

    A.   Elements play a huge part in art in color and design

18. According to the text what is the difference between forced obsolescence and artificial obsolescence?

    A.   Forced obsolescence is the normal course of things for technologies—when thing have run their course. Artificial obsolescence occurs when people want newer, fancier designs like the Joneses.

19. What was Kenneth Parker famous for?

    A.   Kenneth Parker was famous for his luxury Duofold pen.

20. What was used as the tips of his new pens?

    A.   The pen first used a gold tip, replaced by ruthenium tip.

21. As design prophet Moholy-Nagy could have predicted, **fashion** trumped **need**.

22. What was an amazing feat in 1947?

    A. Sales of his pens jumped from 440,000 units to 2.1 million in 1947.

23. Why did the high-end market for Parker 51 begin to shrivel?

    A. The market for the pens began to shrivel because of the arrival of the typewriter.

24. What was the irony about Mark Twain, the pen, and the type-writer?

    A. He was one of the first to buy a typewriter, hated it and gave it away. His first typewritten manuscript, Life on the Missis-sippi, was sent to his publisher. That in itself pushed sales.

25. How did Mark Twain and Goethe feel about humans and their use of technology?

    A. They doubted Homo sapiens had enough wisdom to use technology properly.

26. According to this author how would Mark Twain feel about tech-nology had he lived another 40 years?

    A. He would have felt dispirited with people lusting after nuclear missiles instead of plentiful atomic energy.

27. Describe Robert Lowell's personality.

    A. He could be described as a mad artist.

28. What did pharmaceutical psychology say about Lowell?

    A. It said that Lowell had a chemical imbalance, which rendered him manic-depressive.

29. How does lithium help someone with depression?

   A. Lithium prevents the next episode from starting.

30. What is the difference between so called "normal" people and those with bipolar disorders?

   A. In normal people, ambient conditions, especially the sun, dictate their humors and determine when they are tuckered out. Bi-polar people run on cycles independent of the sun.

31. How do people with "pathological enthusiasm" act?

   A. People with "pathological enthusiasm" barely need sleep, and their self-confidence swells. Those surges deplete the brain and people crash.

31. What are the "black dogs"?

   A. When people crash, the black dogs, they sometimes take to their beds for weeks.

32. **Sunlight** resets the proteins over and over.

33. What is the down side of artists taking lithium?

   A. Many artists feel flatlined or tranquilized on lithium.

34. Lowell's lithium may be a case where it provided **health** but subdued **art**, and made a mad **genius** merely **human**.

CHAPTER 15

1. According to this author what are the differences between mad artists and mad scientists?

    A. Mad scientists of the periodic table had fewer public outbursts than mad artists, and they generally didn't lead notorious private lives either.

2. What spurred Crookes to take up the new movement of spiritualism?

    A. The death of his brother spurred Crookes to spiritualism as a way to handle his grief.

3. Crookes compared himself to a traveler in exotic lands, **Marco Polo** of the paranormal.

4. Explain the relation ship between selenium and 1) AIDS, 2) cattle

    A. The depletion of selenium in the bloodstream of AIDS patients is a fatally accurate harbinger of death. Selenium makes cattle go mad, growing addicted to locoweed.

5. Crookes was the first to suggest the existence of **isotopes**.

6. How do pathological scientists work?

    A. Pathological scientists pick out a marginal and unlikely phenomenon that appeals to them for whatever reason and bring all their scientific acumen to proving its existence

7. Why does our author call paleontology pathological science?

   A. Because there is a very little evidence to support finds, pale-ontologist must extrapolate their evidence by comparing the grooves and depressions on fossilized bones with modern creatures' bones.

8. What did the HMS Challenger dredge up from the ocean floor?

   A. The HMS Challenger dredged up rocks of manganese formed around giant shark teeth, five inches or more from mouths capable of shattering bone like an ax.

9. What did paleontologists determine just from the teeth?

   A. Paleontologist dubbed the find a megalodon that grew to approximately 50 feet, weighed 50 tons and could swim 50 miles per hour.

10. Why could some call this faulty science?

    A. Faulty science exists because without objective evidence, it's not plausible to conclude that megalodons, even a few of them slipped through evolution's snares.

11. Sailors' eyewitness accounts of megalodons are unreliable. Why?

    A. Sailors are notorious storytellers.

12. What argument does people make about the possible existence of megalodons?

    A. People bring up the coelacanth, a primitive deep-sea fish once thought to have gone extinct eighty million years ago, until it turned up in a fish market in South Africa in 1938.

13. What did Pons and Fleischmann think they had discovered when they used a palladium electrode in a current of water?

    A. They thought they had discovered cold fusion.

14. This discovery basically implied that the world's energy problems were **over, cheaply and without pollution.**

15. The two scientists appealed directly to President George H. W. Bush for **$25 million** in immediate research funds.

16. In reality the duo had overlooked **experimental errors** and used faulty **measuring techniques.**

17. Why did their work turn into pathological science?

    A.   The need to believe in clean, cheap energy for the whole world proved tenacious.

18. Why did Rontgen think he had gone stark mad?

    A.   The truly creepy, truly black magic moment came when he held up a plug of metal—and saw the bones of his own hand.

19. How did he skirt pathological science?

    A.   He skirted pathological science with thorough documentation and objective results.

20. What had he discovered?

    A.   He discovered Rontgen rays.

21. Why was Rontgen every scientist's hero?

    A.   Although a middling professor his whole life, he fought back with solid proof, with repeatable experiments.

22. Element #111 became **Roentgenium.**

CHAPTER 16

1. What does extreme cold do to the elements?

    A. Extreme cold hypnotizes elements into strange behaviors.

2. What was the disappointment to Robert Scott when he reached the South Pole?

    A. He lost out to Roald Amundsen, whose team had arrived a month earlier.

3. What conditions did Scott face on this journey?

    A. They were marooned for weeks in a monsoon of snow flurries, and their journals showed that they faced starvation, scurvy, dehydration, hypothermia, and gangrene, and lack of heating fuel.

4. What did he notice about his fuel containers?

    A. They found the canisters awaiting them on the return trip empty and that some of the fuel had leaked into the food.

5. What happened to his team?

    A. They officially died of exposure in late March 1912, eleven miles wide of the British base.

6. What happens to pure tin chemically when it is faced with extreme cold?

    A. Whenever pure tin tools or tin coins or tin toys got cold, whitish rust began to creep over them like hoarfrost on a window in winter. The rust would break out into pustules, then weaken and corrode the tin, until it crumbled and eroded away.

7. At what cold temperature does tin start reacting?

    A. Tin becomes protein at 56 degrees when the pustules rise and the hoarfrost creeps.

8. Why is this condition sometimes called "tin leprosy?"

    A. It is called tin leprosy because it burrows deep inside like a disease.

9. What are 2 examples of the above condition happening?

    A. 1) tin pipes on a new church organ exploding into ash the instant the organist blasted his first chord 2)tin clasps on his men's jackets reportedly cracked apart and left the French-men's inner garments exposed every time the wind kicked up.

10. Why is Jell-O called a hybrid state of matter?

    A. The water and gelatin mixture can either be thought of as a highly flexible solid or a very sluggish liquid.

11. Describe how ice itself has several states of matter.

    A. Scientists coax ice into forming fifteen distinctly shaped crystals by using high-pressure chambers.

12. What was the first noble gas compound created by Neil Bartlett?

    A. He created the first noble gas compound, a solid orange crystal with xenon in 1962, krypton.

13. When was the first krypton solid created?

    A. The first krypton solid was created in 1963.

14. **Argon** wears the title belt for the single hardest element humans have forced into a compound.

15. How are atoms arranged differently in solids, liquids, and gases?

    A. Atoms in solids are fixed in place; liquids particles can flow around each other; and gases, where particles have the freedom to carom about, are distinct states of matter.

16. Explain simply the law of electricity.

    A. Inside a copper wire, the electrons flow between and around the copper atoms, and the wire loses energy as heat when the electrons crash into the atoms.

17. What happens to the electrical current at -450 degrees in a super-conductor?

    A. In fact, the current can flow forever as long as the super conductor remains chilled, a property first detected in mercury at -450 degrees.

18. Who was the BCS theory of superconductivity named after?

    A. BCS theory was named after John Bardeen, Leon Cooper, and Robert Schrieffer.

19. What is wave-particle duality?

    A. Light travels as waves or in particles, BBs, called photons.

20. Lasers use crystals of **yttrium** spiked with **neodymium**.

21. What metaphor is used to describe the action of a laser?

    A. The author uses an elevator as metaphor for a laser.

22. Laser beams are so powerful they can induce **thermonuclear fusion**, yet so focused they **can sculpt a cornea without frying the rest of the eye.**

23. What 2 big names called Charles Townes discovery of masers and then laser impossible?

    A.   John von Neumann and Niels Bohr called Charles Townes discovery masers.

24. So as physicists have done throughout history, Bose decided to pretend that **his error was the truth**, admit that **he didn't know why**, and **write a paper.**

25. Temperature just measures the **average speed of particles**. Hot molecules are **furious little chasing fists**, and cold molecules **drag along.**

26. Scientists might soon be able to build **matter lasers** that shoot out ultra-focused beams of atoms thousands of times more powerful than light laser.

CHAPTER 17

1. One of the most important pieces of scientific equipment in history was invented by a **glass of bee**r.

2. Bubbles in liquids form around **imperfections** or **incongruities**.

3. Bubbles in beer are dissolved pockets of **carbon dioxide**.

4. When do kaons, muons, and pions appear?

    A. Kaons, muons, and pions appear only when an atom's nucleus, its dense core, is splintered.

5. Liquids are thousands of time denser than **gases**.

6. Glaser invented the **bubble chamber**.

7. Liquid hydrogen boils at **-435 degrees F**, so even minute amounts of heat with make **froth**.

8. What do biologists use bubbles to study?

    A. Biologists use bubbles to study the development of cells, the most complex structures in the universe.

9. What is foam?

    A. Foam develops when bubbles overlap and lose their spherical shape.

10. Calcium-enriched bones are both **strong** yet **light**.

11. Rainwater and calcium form **huge cavities, caves**.

12. English limestone has built what buildings?

    A.   English limestone has built Buckingham Palace, the Tower of   London, and Westminster Abbey.

13. What is the relationship between froth and Benjamin Franklin and froth and Robert Boyle?

    A.   Benjamin Franklin who discovered why oil calms frothy water and Robert Boyle who experimented and even liked to taste the fresh, frothy urine in the chamber pot.

14. What are "intuitive sciences"?

    A.   Intuitive sciences investigate natural phenomena that relied on hunches and almanacs instead of controlled experiments.

15. What intuitive science picked up the study of bubbles?

    A.   The intuitive science that picked up bubble research was cooking.

16. What do chefs and chemists distrust each other?

    A.   Chemists see cooks as undisciplined and unscientific, cooks seeing chemists as sterile killjoys.

17. What men are responsible for bubble science?

    A.   Ernest Rutherford and Lord Kelvin are responsible for bubble science.

18. Helium **glows** when excited by electricity.

19. What is the feat of progeny of Genghis Khan?

    A.   Khan fathered hundreds of children.

20. How did William Thomson come to the conclusion that earth was twenty million years old?

    A. Thomson measured the rate of lost heat and extrapolating backward to when every rock on earth was molten, they could estimate the earth's date of origin.

21. Lots of **helium** inside a rock means that it's **old**, while scant traces it's a **youngster**.

22. Rutherford discovered element 104, **rutherfordium**.

23. Zirconium is best known for **fake diamonds**.

24. How do scientists determine the world's oldest rock?

    A. Scientists use zircon-uranium bubbles to date it.

25. Lord Kelvin popularized **froth science**.

26. D'Arcy Wentworth Thompson published what book that was called "the finest work of literature . . . "

27. Why did WWI submarine propellers disintegrate and decay?

    A. It turned out that bubbles produced by the churning propellers turned around and attacked the metal blades like sugar attacks teeth, and with similarly corrosive results.

28. What is sonoluminescence?

    A. When bubbles appeared would sometimes collapse and wink at them with a flash of blue or green light.

29. "Singularity" is usually associated with **black holes**.

30. Why is AIDS a foamy virus?

    A. AIDS was called a foamy virus for the way infected cells swell before exploding.

31. What is the relationship between bubbles and insects and bubbles and peacocks?

    A.   Entomologists know of insects that use bubbles like submersibles to breathe underwater, and ornithologists know that the metallic sheen of peacock's feathers plumage comes from light tickling bubbles in the feathers.

32. What makes Diet Coke explode when you drop a Mentos candy?

    A.   Mentos candy acts as a net to snag small dissolved bubbles, which are stitched into large ones. Eventually, a few gigantic bubbles break off, rocket upward, and whoosh through the nozzle.

CHAPTER 18

1. What is the purpose of the standards bureau?

    A. The job of the standards bureau is to measure everything.

2. What is the BIPM and where is it located?

    A. BIPM is the Bureau of International de Poids Mesures just outside Paris that acts as the standards bureau, making sure all franchises stay in line.

3. The Kilogram is made of dense **platinum.** What are 3 reasons this is used?

    A. It is used to minimize the surface area exposed to unacceptably dirty air. It also conducts electricity well and the toughness mitigates against the chance of a disastrous fingernail nick.

4. Define calibration.

    A. To fix the graduations of a measuring instrument.

5. Why is flying K20 to Paris an absolute hassle?

    A. It is a hassle since 2001 because they have to hand carry the kilograms through the flight, and it's hard to get through security and customs with a slug of metal, and tell people they cannot touch it.

6.　Where are copies of the Kilogram kept?

A.　Six official copies of the Kilogram are kept under two bell jars to calibrate the knock offs.

7.　What does science owe much of its progress to since 1600?

A.　Much of the progress of science is due to adopting an objective non-human centered point of view about the universe.

8.　The Copernican principle is also called **mediocrity principle**.

9.　The kilogram is one of **seven base units** of measurement.

10.　Measurement scientists have redefined a meter as **the distance any light travels in a vacuum in 1/299,792,458** of a second.

11.　What is a "leap" second?"

A.　A leap second is added every third year because the sloshing of ocean tides drag and slow earth's rotation.

12.　Explain how atomic clocks run.

A.　Atomic clocks run on the same leaping crashing of excited electrons.

13.　Why was cesium convenient as the mainspring for atomic clocks?

A.　It was convenient because it has one electron exposed in its outermost shell, with no nearby electrons to muffle it.

14.　How fast is a cesium electron?

A.　It performs 9,192,631,770 back-and-forth every one Mississippi.

15.　Cesium may be a fine element but it lacks the **mythic feeling of the moon or sun.**

16 .The best-known dimensionless constant is the **fine structure constant, which is related to the fine splitting of electrons**.

17. **Arthur Eddington**, who during a solar eclipse in 1919 provided the first experimental proof of **Einstein's relativity**, grew fascinated with **alpha**.

18. Today alpha makes the periodic table possible. How?

    A.   Alpha allows atoms to exist and also allows them to react with sufficient vigor to form compounds, since electrons neither roam too freely from their nuclei nor cling too closely.

19. Alexander Shlyakhter scrutinized a bizarre site in **Africa** called **Oklo** and declared that alpha was getting **bigger**.

20. Oklo was powered by nothing but **uranium, water**, and **blue-green algae**.

21. For a chain reaction to occur, neutron must not only strike uranium nuclei, they must **absorb them**.

22. Star systems are called **quasars** and **interstellar** dust clouds.

23. Quasars are **black stars** that tear apart and **cannibalize** other stars.

24. Enrico Fermi died of **beryllium poisoning** after some brash experiments and won a Nobel Prize for discovering **transuranic elements** he really didn't discover.

25. What assignment did Fermi ask his students to perform?

    A.   He asked his students to figure out how many millimeters thick the duct could get on the famously dirty windows in his lab before the dust avalanched under its own weight and sloughed onto the floor.

26. What is the Drake Equation?

    A. This equation is a series of guesses; about how many stars exit in the galaxy, what fraction of those have earthlike planets, what fraction of those planets have intelligent life, what fraction of those life forms would want to make contact.

27. Why is the Drake Equation important?

    A. It outlines what data astronomers need to collect, and it put astrobiology on a scientific foundation.

28. If scientists were looking for life on another planet, what element might they search for?

    A. They might search for elements such as magnesium.

29. Almost all life forms use **metallic elements** in trace amounts. Animals primarily use the i**ron** in **hemoglobin.**

30. **Chlorophyll** is probably the most important organic chemical on earth because it drives **photosynthesis** by converting **stellar** energy into sugars, the basis of the food chain.

31. Magnesium in animals helps **DNA** function properly.

32. Magnesium on planets implies the presence of **bacteria.** How does magnesium help maintain a liquid ocean?

    A. Magnesium salts depress the freezing point of water so that it stays liquid at lower temperatures.

33. Einstein determined that space and time are **intertwined**.

34. Discovering life on other planets would be proof the human beings **are not so special after all**.

CHAPTER 19

1.   Using context clues from the first paragraph define conundrum.

   A.   Conundrum is a paradox or mystery.

2.   **90%** of the particles in the universe are **hydrogen,** and the other **10%** are **helium**.

3.   Astatine is the scarcest natural element. What metaphor is used to describe this scarcity?

   A.   The metaphor is trying to find a car in 160 identical garages with 100 million spaces, 100 million rows, and 100 million spaces high.

4.   How does astatine still exist if its radioactivity has disintegrated?

   A.   Other radioactive elements sometimes decay into astatine after they split out alpha or beta particles.

5.   What is astatine good for?

   A.   It is good as a quick-acting radioisotope in medicine.

6.   Astatine remains the only element whose discovery was confirmed by a **nonprimate**.

7.   **Uranium** is more stable than either astatine or **francium**.

8.   Attempts to reach the oasis of **superheavy elements** have made up one of the most exciting fields of physics.

9.   To get truly stable, doubly magic elements, they need to figure out ways to add more n**eutrons** to their targets.

10. Why is francium more abundant than astatine?

     A.   Francium is more abundant than astatine because many radioactive elements around uranium happen to decay into francium as they disintegrate.

11. The binomial species system in biology is gradually being replaced by **chromosomal DNA bar codes**. Instead of Home sapiens, hello TCATCGGTCATTGG. . . .

12. Einstein actually won his Nobel Prize for **explaining a strange effect in quantum mechanics, the photoelectric effect**.

13. What is the "theory of everything"?

     A.   Trying to unify quantum mechanics and relativity into a coherent and svelte.

14. Richard Feynman called **alpha** one of the great damn mysteries of the universe.

15. What did Glenn Seaborg and his colleagues accomplish?

     A.   They made over the entire periodic table between the late 1930s and early 1960s.

16. What are superatoms?

     A.   Superatoms are clusters between 8 and 10 atoms of one element.

17. What is jellium?

    A. Jellium is when atoms arrange themselves into a three-dimensional polyhedron, and each atom in it mimics a proton or neutron in a collective nucleus.

18. A quantum dot is a **sort of holographic virtual atom**. An example of a quantum dot is **indium**.

19 .Explain in detail Devils Tower.

    A. The tower consists of layers—from the bottom up, there's a semiconductor, a thin layer of an insulator (a ceramic), indium, a thicker layer of a ceramic, and a cap of metal on top.

20. Who does our author want to donate $1,000?

    A. The author wants to donate $1000 to some nonprofit group to support tinkering with wild new periodic tables based on whatever organizing principles people can imagine.

PEMBROKE NOTES

Common Core and Alaska State Standards

Reading Informational Text

1.   Cite strong and thorough textural evidence to support analysis of what the text says explicitly as well as implicit inferences drawn from the text.

2.   Determine a central idea of a text and analyze its development over the course of the text, including how it emerges and is shaped and refined by specific details: restate and summarize main ideas or events, in correct sequence when necessary, after reading the text.

3.   Analyze in detail how an author's ideas or claims are developed and refined by particular sentences, paragraphs, or larger portions of a text.

4.   Determine an author's point of view on purpose in a text and analyze how an author uses rhetoric to advance that point of view or purpose.

5.   Delineate and evaluate the argument and specific claims in a text.

Writing Standards

1. Write informative/explanatory texts to examine and convey complex ideas, concepts, and information clearly and accurately through the effective selection, organization, and analysis of content.

2. Produce clear and coherent writing in which the development, organization, style, and features are appropriate to task, genre, purpose, and audience.

3. Use technology, including the Internet, to produce, publish, and update individual or shared writing products, taking advantage of technology's capacity to line to other information to display information flexibly and dynamically.

4. Draw evidence from literary or informational texts to support analysis reflection, and research.

5. Write routinely over extended time frames (time for research, reflection, and revision) and shorter time frames (a single sitting a day or two) for a range of tasks, and issues, building on others' ideas and expressing their own clearly and persuasively.

Language Standards

1. Demonstrate command of the conventions of standard English, capitalization, punctuation, and spelling when writing.

2. Apply knowledge of language of language to understand how language functions in different contexts, to make effective choices for meaning or style, and comprehend more fully when reading or listening.

3. Determine or clarify the meaning of unknown and multiple-meaning words and phrases based on grades 9-12 reading and content, choosing flexibly from a range of strategies.

WRITING WORKSHOP

THE ARGUMENT ESSAY

OVERVIEW	IMPORTANT ELEMENTS	TOPIC SELECTION
In preparing our students for college it is important to know that the argument essay may be one of the most common writing assignment they may encounter.	**Perform effective and thorough research** before committing to a topic to ensure enough credible resources for support. **Effective thesis statement** is important in any essay but especially important for the argument essay because the writer needs to identify the argument and why the argument is important. This cannot be confusing to the reader. **Necessary background information on the topic** supplies the needed details to support the thesis statement Because the argument essay involves multiple reasons and evidence to support overall thesis statement the writer should **focus on organization and transitions.** **Incorporate logos, pathos, and ethos** throughout the essay. Although logos (logic) should be the primary focus, pathos (emotion) can also be used for the argument essay. Ethos (credibility) is addressed by addressing counter arguments and using credible sources	**Current, debatable, researchable, and manageable** topics are best to use for the argument essay because they can be argued logically. A **current** topic is one that has not been over-debated and is still being decided. Avoid topics such as abortion, the death penalty, the legalization of marijuana. A **debatable** topic is controversial with differing viewpoints. Writing about domestic violence is not debatable since no one would disagree with this thesis. But debating whether common punishments for domestic violence are effective and a deterrent. A **researchable topic** can be supported with a variety of credible and current sources. A **manageable topic** is one that has been narrowed enough to meet the page requirement of the essay. Begin with a basic broad subject and then narrow it down to a subtopic.

CAUSE EFFECT ESSAY

OVERVIEW	TIPS
These essays are not to be about both causes and effects, but a focus on either cause or effect	**Introduction**—let your audience know what you are going write about. **Keep a narrow topical focus** and don't try to answer all causes or effects. Three or four is a good number to concentrate on. **Support all causes or effects with supporting details.** **Decide on the order in which to present information.** **Conclusion**—restate thesis or generalize your essay

COMPARE CONTRAST ESSAY

OVERVIEW	TIPS
These essays are huge in academic writing. They will follow a specific question and are fairly easy to complete. It is important to remember the structure and keep it consistent.	**Introduction**—like a five-paragraph essay, use a quotation, anecdote, generalization and then lead into the thesis statement. **Topic 1**—cover only the first topic of the comparison and contrast. Do not mention topic 2 in the first part. **Topic 2**—cover the second of the two topics. Do not discuss topic 1 here. **Topics 1 & 2 together**—Now analyze both topics together in one or multiple paragraphs. **Conclusions**—should be a generalization of the thesis as in introduction. Reaffirm your thesis. You complete knowledge of the subject should be apparent.

THE EVALUATION ESSAY

OVERVIEW	IMPORTANT ELEMENTS	TOPIC SELECTION
The purpose of an evaluation essay is to demonstrate the overall quality (or lack thereof) of a particular product, business, place, service, or program. While opinions are interjected naturally in this essay, if done properly the evaluation should seem reasoned and unbiased.	An overall **thesis** should be offered. Having clear **criteria** (ideal for the product/place/service/etc.) is what keeps an evaluation from feeling less like an opinion. The **judgment** is the establishment of whether or not the criterion is met. In other words, the judgment is what actually is. The **evidence** is the details offered to support the judgment Each body paragraph of an evaluation should **focus on one specific criterion,** which should be fully explained, followed by the judgment and a variety of evidence offered as support. Consequently all evaluations should contain several **different** criteria, judgments, and evidence	Focus on **specific business, service, product, or policy.** Write about a topic that you **have knowledge about** to make it easier to establish the appropriate criteria, judgments, and evidence.

THE INVESTIGATIVE ESSAY

OVERVIEW	IMPORTANT ELEMENTS	TOPIC SELECTION
Although similar to an argumentative essay, an investigative essay is often a precursor to an argument. The investigative essay allows for opinions and personal experiences, a difference from the argument essay.	In order to demonstrate a thorough knowledge of the subject, the writer **researches, researches, researches.** Writer must expertly interpret **research** and **articulate the various viewpoints** of the issue. The best investigative essays begin with a **legitimate question** to research, one that the writer is exploring.	**Current, debatable, researchable, and manageable** topics are best to use for the argument essay because they can be argued logically. A **current** topic is one that has not been over-debated and is still being decided. Avoid topics such as abortion, the death penalty, the legalization of marijuana. A **debatable** topic is controversial with differing viewpoints. Writing about domestic violence is not debatable since no one would disagree with this thesis. But debating whether common punishments for domestic violence are effective and a deterrent. A **researchable topic** can be supported with a variety of credible and current sources. A **manageable topic** is one that has been narrowed enough to meet the page requirement of the essay. Begin with a basic broad subject and then narrow it down to a subtopic.

PERSONAL ESSAY

OVERVIEW	TIPS
Often incorporating a variety of writing styles, the personal essay asks the writer to write about an important person, event, or time period in his/her life. The goal is to narrate this event in a way that uses both narrative and descriptive writing, which are two of the main models in writing.	**Focus on detail**—show, not tell using strong verbs, not overusing adjectives. **Use sensory detail**—bring the reader farther by using a variety of senses: sound, smell, touch, taste, in addition to sight. **Connect the event/person/place to a larger idea**—don't lose focus on the main idea: how the event changed you. It's the importance of the event that counts. **Be careful with verb tense**—when in doubt, stick with **past** tense for the actual event and **present** tense to discuss the change.

RESPONDING TO AN ESSAY

OVERVIEW	APPROACHES
Often following a literature summary, the writer responds to the piece subjectively using well -supported opinions and personal experiences. The thesis is the overall opinion of the essay you are responding to. Always be specific and always have support.	Agree or disagree with **the author's main point or thesis.** Agree or disagree with **the extent to which the thesis is made.** Agree or disagree with **specific points that are made that relate to the thesis.** Agree or disagree with **specific evidence that is offered in support of the thesis** Agree or disagree with **the relevancy of the overall topic.**

SUMMARIZING

OVERVIEW	TIPS
Although the shortest piece of writing in a high school course, it is not easy. A good summary accurately describes the main point and important details of the piece. In order to be accurate and concise the writer must be thoroughly familiar with the original work. If too long, a summary may be paraphrasing the original work, bit if too short, important details may be left out. Think one quarter to one third of the total length of the original article.	Read and **reread** essay as many times as necessary to gain a full understanding of it. No **first person statements** allowed. Opinions are not needed here. **Always name the author and article title** in the introductory paragraph, usually in the first or second sentence. From then on refer to author by **last name.** **Always use present tense** to discuss the essay and facts from the essay. Use **direct quotes or paraphrase** examples to support your claims. When talking about an essay or article, **always capitalize the title and place it in quotation marks.** Do not use italics.

CPSIA information can be obtained at www.ICGtesting.com
Printed in the USA
LVOW07s0450220615

443347LV00001B/81/P